HEADWAY ENGLISH

By Howell Moses

Designed by
Lloyd Fishwick Associates

COLLINS EDUCATIONAL

Acknowledgements
Illustrations by Toni Goffe p26, 38, 39; Mark Hudson p64; Michael Strand p73;
Pat Tourret p57, 72; Wendi Watson p74; Barry Wilkinson p32, 33.

The author and publishers would like to thank the following for
permission to reproduce photographs:
Ancient Art and Architecture Collection p44;
J Allan Cash p36, 45, 52;
BBC Hulton Picture Library p60;
British Tourist Authority p34 (far left);
European Parliament Information Office p6;
Keith Gibson p21;
Help the Aged/Whitecross School p34 (top);
Bob Langrish p53, 62 (top);
Irish Tourist Board p4, 5, 11, front cover;
John Mannion p14, 62 (bottom);
Manpower Services Commission p30, 40, 42, 43, 48, 49, 50, 71, cover;
The Mansell Collection p37 (top);
Marion and Tony Morrison p84, 85;
Howell Moses p12 (top), 13 (top);
Netherlands Tourist Board p68 (right);
Drangways Restaurant p21;
The Photo Source p68 (left);
Popperfoto p60, 61;
Promotion Australia, London p76, 77, back cover;
John Rae, p16, 20, 34 (x3), 78, 79;
J Sainsbury Plc p23;
Vidal Sassoon p43, front cover;
Scottish Tourist Board p37 (bottom), 69;
Swiss Tourist Board p58;
Thomson Directories p17;
Trust House Forte Times p7, 24, 25;
Welsh Folk Museum p12, 13 (bottom).

Every effort has been made to contact the copyright holders, but in some
cases this has been impossible. It is hoped that any omissions will be excused.

© 1987 Howell Moses
0 00 323004 X
Published by Collins Educational
77-85 Fulham Palace Road, Hammersmith, London W6 8JB
First impression 1987
Reprinted 1989
Reprinted 1991

Printed and bound in Great Britain by Scotprint Ltd, Musselburgh

All rights reserved.
No part of this publication may be reproduced, stored in a retrieval system, or transmitted, in any form or by any means,
electronic, mechanical, photocopying, recording or otherwise, without the prior permission of the copyright owner.

Contents

Shark Fishing

Shark fishing began in Britain and Ireland just over sixty years ago. Kinsale in Ireland and Looe in Cornwall are two places where people fish for sharks.

The shark most often caught is the blue shark. It has a long thin body and a long pointed fin. The upper surface of the body is silvery-blue. This colour fades until, on the underside, the body is pure white. In warm tropical waters the blue shark grows to a length of over six metres. They turn the scales at around one hundred and sixty kilogrammes. However, even a good specimen taken from the waters around Kinsale and Looe will only be about two metres long and weigh around twenty-five kilogrammes.

Sharks appear in these northern waters from April to September. They arrive at the same time as huge shoals of pilchard and mackerel, the fish on which the shark feed.

Sea anglers fish for shark with a rod and line. Their bait is a bag of ruddy-duddy. This is a mixture of chopped pilchard and mackerel. The dripping bag, held at the side of the boat, leaves an oily trail which attracts the shark.

Read about shark fishing off the coast of Britain and Ireland than answer the questions.

1 Where in Britain and Ireland has shark fishing become a sport?

2 Name and describe the kind of shark most often seen in these areas.

3 During what period of the year are the sharks caught?

4 What is the name given to a fisherman who uses a rod and line?

5 What bait is used by shark fishermen?

6 What is the bait called?

7 How does it attract the shark?

8 Explain these phrases:

    a They turn the scales
    b a good specimen.
    c huge shoals.

9 Which word is used to describe a large number of mackerel?

Word Work

1   <u>ABBREVIATIONS</u>

Some titles and names are often shortened when they are written or spoken.

JP	— stands for —	Justice of the Peace
MP		Member of Parliament

When this happens, the shortened form of the title or word is called its ABBREVIATION.

---

2   <u>POINTS OF THE COMPASS</u>   ASSIGNMENT 2

Draw a compass in your book.
Write in the correct position, the abbreviation and the name of each position in full.

North, South, East, West,
North-East, South-West,
South-East, North-West.

---

3   <u>ABOUT TOWN</u>   ASSIGNMENT 3

Match each of these abbreviations with the words in full.

St. Ave. Rd. Cres. Sq.
Avenue Square Crescent Road Street.

---

4   <u>WEIGHTS AND MEASURES</u>   ASSIGNMENT 4

Now do the same for these abbreviations

m.p.h. hp cc r.p.m. £
kg approx. est. km yd.
ft. cm. gall. doz. qr. lb.

foot yard pound (money) horsepower
cubic capacity approximately miles per hour
revolutions per minute kilogram estimate
centimetre gallon quarter kilometre
dozen pound (weight)

Can you think of any other abbreviations which you have met in maths lessons?

ABBREVIATION

abbrev., abbreviation.
A.D., Anno Domini.
agric., agricultural.
alt., altitude.
a.m., ante meridiem (before noon).
anc., ancient, anciently.
A.R.A., Associate of the Royal Academy.
A.S., Anglo-Saxon.
A.V., Authorised Version

b., born.
Bart., Bt., Baronet.
B.C., Before Christ.
bor., borough. [dies.
B.W.I., British West In-

C., Centigrade.
c., circa (about).
Captain.

E., east, eastern.
eccles., ecclesiastical.
ed., edited, edition.
e.g., exempli gratia (for example).
E.M.F., electromotive force.
Eng., English.
episc., episcopal.
E.R., East Riding (Yorkshire).
etc., et cetera.
et seq., et sequens (and the following).

F., Fahrenheit.
fig., figure.
Fr., French.
F.R.S., Fellow of the Royal Society.
ft., feet.

ib.,
id.,
i.e.,
i.h.
illu
in-
isl.
Ita

J.

j

5

Copy these words into your notebook:

    valuable   vague   frowned   censored
    miserable   novel   hostile   whisper

Fit one of the above words into each of the sentences below.

1   Sanji wore a .... bracelet around his wrist.
2   When the police arrived they were met by a ....
     crowd.
3   Mary gave the police a .... description
     of the youths.
4   Paul and Sandra had a .... holiday in Scarborough.
5   Karl came up with a .... idea for saving the club.
6   Tracey was able to .... instructions to her rescuers.
7   The warder passed the .... letters to the prisoners.
8   The waiter .... as he served the coffee to the guests.

6

Rewrite these sentences.
This time complete each of the above sentences with a word which is opposite in meaning to the one above.

7

Words which begin with the prefix
MONO are all linked with the idea of one.

A MONOPLANE is an aeroplane
with one pair of wings.

Look up the meaning of these words in your dictionary:

monochrome monocle monogamy monogram

Write the word and its meaning in your notebook.
Write four sentences.
Use one of the words in each sentence.

Kinds of Poetry

THE NARRATIVE POEM

Sometimes a poem tells a story of a great local or national event,
such as a battle, an accident or the crowning of a king.
Poems which tell stories or recount experiences are called
NARRATIVE POEMS.

Here is an example of a narrative poem.
It tells the story of the terrible explosion
which took place at Gresford Colliery in Clwyd,
North Wales in 1934.

THE GRESFORD DISASTER

You've heard of the Gresford disaster,
The terrible price that was paid,
Two hundred and forty-two colliers were lost
And three men of the rescue brigade.

It occurred in the month of September,
At three in the morning, that pit
Was wracked by a violent explosion
In the Dennis where gas lay so thick.

The gas in the Dennis deep section
Was packed there like snow in a drift,
And many a man had to leave the coal face
Before he had worked out his shift.

A fortnight before the explosion,
To the shot-firer Tomlinson they cried,
'If you fire that shot we'll all blown to hell'
And no one can now say that they lied.

The fireman's reports they are missing,
The records of forty-two days,
The colliery manager had them destroyed
To cover his criminal ways.

Down there in the dark they are lying,
They died for nine shillings a day,
They have worked out their shift
    and now they must lie
In the darkness until Judgement Day.

The Lord Mayor of London's collecting,
To help both our children and wives,
The owners have sent some white lilies,
To pay for the poor collier's lives.

Farewell, our dear wives and our children,
Farewell, our old comrades as well,
Don't send your sons down the dark dreary pit,
They'll be dammed like the sinners in hell.

Writing Work

Either tell the story of the disaster in your own words
or
Pretend you are a newspaper reporter.
Write the story that goes with this headline.

GRESFORD MANAGER TO BE CHARGED – MINE SAFETY NEGLECTED

Read the above poem again, then answer these
questions.
1 What do these words and phrases mean?
   collier rescue brigade wracked dreary.
2 Where is Gresford?
   When did the explosion occur?
   How many men lost their lives?
3 What caused the disaster?
   Who fired the shot that caused the gas to explode?
4 What action did the pit manager take to cover up
   his neglect of safety measures?

Write a narrative poem of your own.
Write about something that has happened to you.
or
Look in newspapers or listen to the news.
Choose one of the items as a subject for your poem.

Reading for Meaning

PERIOD OFFICE BUILDING

Approx. 2,000 s ft. On-site car parking. Full refurbished. Exposed beams 500 pax. Rental £ 500 pax.

FREEHOLD OFFICE BUILDING

HOUSE FOR SALE

Goddard and Co.
Tel. Newport 1234
NEWPORT, Lynwood Ave. Good sized semi-det house on main rd. Good views and open aspect at rear. Close to shops. 10 min bus to town centre. Recently renovated. Full gas CH. Accommodation — porch, ent. hall, lounge 4m × 6m, fully-fitted kitchen, small cloak-room with WC, separate dining-room. 3 bedrooms. Combined WC and bathroom. Extensive garden at rear. Price incl. all carpets, ex-cept lounge. Appt to view from agents. £40 000 ono.

PRESTIGIOUS NEW OFFICE BUILDING

Approx. 4,000 sq. ft., or will divide
Car parking. Fully carpeted. Prominent location.

MODERN SHOP PREMISES

NEW INSTRUCTIONS

1. HENLEY RO
   General Store
   accomm
   £50,000 –

2. BRAMFORD
   Hairdressers
   above. Appr
   £57,500 –

3. FROBISHER
   Fish and chip
   accommo
   Rent £

4. STOKE
   Modern shop
   Rent

5. UPLAND
   Contractor's
   Gross area
   carpeting,
   availa

To save space, advertisements for houses often contain
several abbreviations.
Find out the meaning of these abbreviations:
ono CH ent WC incl appt

Read these phrases.
Write in your book those that correctly describe the house:
stands on its own
is joined to one other house
is part of a row of houses
is in a quiet street
is on a main road
takes half an hour to get into town
can walk into town centre
there are no shops near
the lounge is square shaped
dining area is part of lounge
house needs painting and decorating
there is a large garden
this garden is at the rear of the house

Describe how you would set about making
arrangements to see the inside of the house.
Write a letter to the Estate Agent making an offer
to buy the house.

PUZZLE PAGE

Obtain a copy of this puzzle from your teacher.
(Headway English Copymasters 5, number 1. Extra
puzzles numbers 2 and 3.)
Complete the crossword.

Clues across.
3 Irish fishing centre
5 Hot and cold (Abbrev.)
6 Unfriendly
8 Used to lure or attract
9 Not definite
11 Precious stone
15 Works in a mine
17 Street (Abbrev.)
19 Fisherman's equipment
20 Circus entertainer
21 To carry across

Clues down
1 Oily type of fish
2 Late – anagram
4 Small particle
7 Side (in sport)
9 Calf meat
10 Organ of hearing
12 New, original
13 The back
14 Compass point
16 Opposite of subtract
18 Female sheep (plural)
26 Automobile

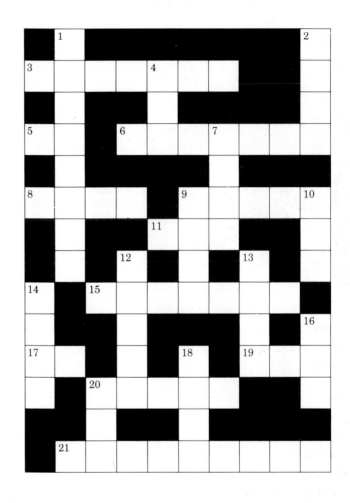

Carved Messages Of Love

These beautifully carved spoons are called love spoons. Men carved them as presents for their girl friends. Giving a spoon as a token of love began about three hundred years ago. The tradition continues today in Wales, Norway, Sweden and several other European countries.

The acceptance of a spoon was a sign that a marriage proposal would be accepted. The decorations on the spoon represent messages to the recipient. A horseshoe is the sign of good luck. A set of keys, means the man is offering a woman the keys to his heart. The spade is the symbol of hard work. In carving the spade, the man is promising to work hard to support his future wife and family.

Love spoons are always carved from a single piece of wood. Making them requires a great deal of skill, time and patience. Sycamore is the wood most carvers prefer, but oak, apple and yew are sometimes chosen.

Traditionally, carved spoons were only given as tokens of love. Today a present of a spoon is given to mark a special occasion, such as a birthday or Christmas. It can also be given to mark a special wedding anniversary.

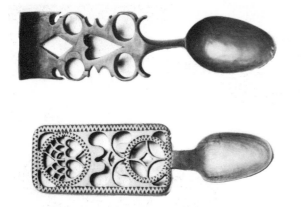

Read about the practice of carving spoons as tokens of love, then answer the following questions.

1 When did the practice of giving a carved spoon as a love token begin?

2 In which countries is the practice still continued?

3 Who were given the spoons?

4 What did it mean if the spoon was accepted?

5 What kind of wood is most suitable for carving?

6 In more recent times, what occasions are marked by the giving of a spoon?

7 In the decoration of a spoon, what special meaning is attached to the carving of:
a spade   a horseshoe   a set of keys?

8 French is the language spoken in France. What language is spoken in:
Germany Spain Italy Norway Sweden Denmark?

9 Find words in the passage which have a similar sound to the following:
cymbal peace would quays thyme you

10 Use your dictionary to find the meaning of these words:
symbol token recipient

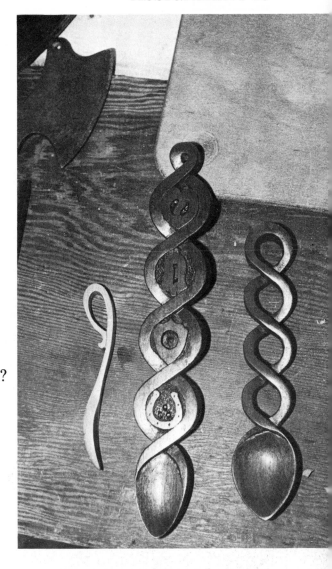

Either copy the drawing of the love spoons or design a spoon of your own.

Write a description of one of the spoons or of your own spoon.

13

LIFE SKILLS

ABOUT TELEVISION

Pretend you have decided to buy a television.
After visiting PLANET ELECTRICS, you decide to buy
the television seen opposite.
At the store, you are asked to fill in an ORDER FORM.
Obtain a copy of this form from your teacher and complete it.
(Headway English Copymasters 5, number 4)

You will be paying cash for the television.
Arrange to have your set delivered next Wednesday,
after 4.30 pm.

**INTERCONTINENTAL
TELEVISION
WORLDWIDE PICTURES
LIFELIKE COLOUR**

20in. screen.
Guaranteed 5 yrs.
Easy to operate.

Comes complete with **remote
control** and internal aerial.

Colour finish—white
walnut

PLANET PRICE £250
Model No: NCJ 2245

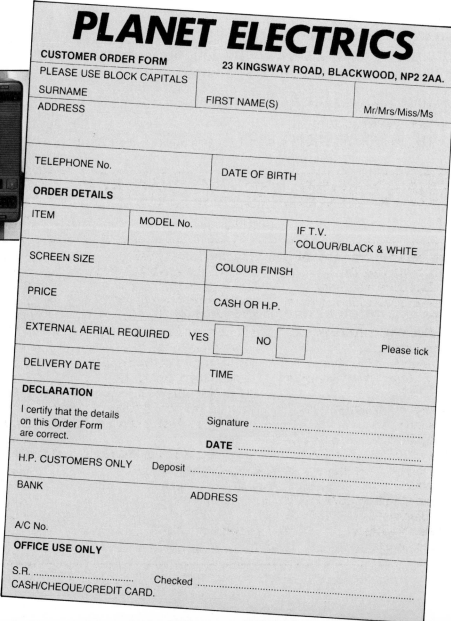

PLANET ELECTRICS

CUSTOMER ORDER FORM   23 KINGSWAY ROAD, BLACKWOOD, NP2 2AA.

PLEASE USE BLOCK CAPITALS

SURNAME   FIRST NAME(S)   Mr/Mrs/Miss/Ms

ADDRESS

TELEPHONE No.   DATE OF BIRTH

ORDER DETAILS

ITEM   MODEL No.   IF T.V.
                             COLOUR/BLACK & WHITE

SCREEN SIZE   COLOUR FINISH

PRICE   CASH OR H.P.

EXTERNAL AERIAL REQUIRED   YES [ ]   NO [ ]
                                              Please tick

DELIVERY DATE   TIME

DECLARATION

I certify that the details
on this Order Form   Signature ....
are correct.
                       DATE ....

H.P. CUSTOMERS ONLY   Deposit ....

BANK
                       ADDRESS

A/C No.

OFFICE USE ONLY

S.R. ....   Checked ....
CASH/CHEQUE/CREDIT CARD.

LIFE SKILLS

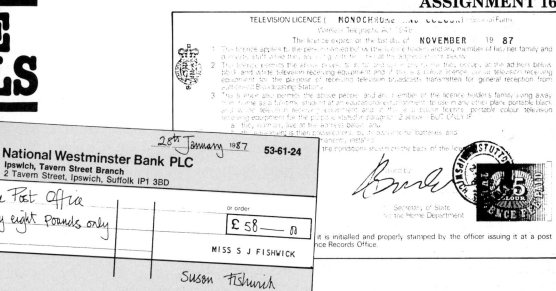

In order to use your television set you will need to buy
a television licence.
Find out the cost of a licence.
Write a cheque for this amount.
Make your cheque payable to the Post Office.

ASSIGNMENT 17

Almost all newspapers publish details
of television programmes.
Look at the programme details then answer the questions on page 16.

YOUR GUIDE TO TO-NIGHT'S TV VIEWING

BBC 1

6.0 **News, Weather** Regional News
6.30 **The Chimp Family**
7.15 **The Dave Jones Show**
8.15 **Film**—Escape to the Sun with Jon Driscoll
9.0 **Main Evening News** Reports from Home and Abroad
9.30 **One Man and His Dog** International Sheepdog trials from Penrith.
10.00 **To-morrows World.** Can computers ever think?
10.45 **Party Political Broadcast** on behalf of the Conservative Party.
11.00 **Highlights** of To-day's skating championships.
11.30 **Come Dancing** from the Tower Ballroom, Blackpool.
12.10 **News, Weather.**
12.20 **Close Down.**

BBC 2

6.0 **Film** Barnaby Farm
7.15 **What's it worth?** Antiques
8.0 **Royal Heritage** Inside Buckingham Palace.
9.0 **Pied Piper.** Fact or fiction.
9.30 **International Snooker** from Birmingham.
10.15 **To-day in the House** Parliamentary round up.
11.00 **The Late Film** – Rocky Rides Again, a Western thriller.
12.00 **News Headlines** Tomorrows weather.
12.15 **Finals** of the World Ice Skating Championships.
1.30 **Close down.**

ITV LONDON

5.0 **London To-day.** Capital reports.
6.30 **Money Box** Advice to savers
6.45 **Pop music quiz**
7.15 **Petticoat lane** ITV's latest soap opera
7.45 **Party Political Broadcast** on behalf of the Labour Party
8.00 **Gardener's World** from Ashton Down Bristol.
8.30 **Royal Command Performance** from the London Palladium.
9.30 **News**
9.45 **Tales of Intrigue.** Who killed Baroness Box?
10.30 **Late Film.** Princess of Power.
12.00 **Tomorrows Headlines.** A look at tomorrow's papers.
12.20 **Close Down**

LIFE SKILLS

1 The letters BBC and ITV are abbreviations for the names of the two television companies. Write the names of the companies in full.

2 ITV is called a commercial company. What does this mean?

3 LONDON ITV is one of the commercial companies in the London area. What is the name of the commercial company which can be seen in your area?

4 On which channel and at what time could you see these programmes:
   a Sheepdog Trials
   b A Western thriller
   c A programme about gardening?

5 Which group of sportspeople are likely to watch the programme on BBC 2 at 9.30 p.m.?

6 What is a 'soap opera'? What is the name of the soap opera to be seen on ITV? Can you name any other soap operas to be seen on television?

7 What is a party political broadcast? To which channel would you turn and at what time to hear about the policies of the Labour Party?

8 Some people like to collect antiques. What are antiques? Which programme would be of special interest to antique collectors?

9 You would need to stay up until what time to see the finals of the World Ice-Skating Championships?

10 If you decided not to watch Snooker from Birmingham, what other programmes could you choose?

ASSIGNMENT 18

Television Diary
Make a list of some of the programmes you have watched recently on television.
Write what you thought of the programmes.

LIFE SKILLS

ASSIGNMENT 19

Unfortunately your television set develops a fault soon after it is installed.

You look in a local directory for PLANET ELECTRICS. For some reason, the names of the television repair firms have not been listed in alphabetical order.

Read the list of firms and arrange them in alphabetical order.

Dependable TV Services, 28 Abbey Rd ....
Comet Electrics, 34 High Street ....
Edwards Eric, 112 St John's St ....
Planet Electrics, 23 Kingsway Rd ....
Highland Electrical Services, 3 The Fairfax ....
Morgans Television Ltd, 31 Albert Rd ....

ASSIGNMENT 20

Write a letter to the Servicing Department of PLANET ELECTRICS.

Tell them that your television has broken down.

Ask them to send round their repair person.

Suggest a date and time when this would be convenient.

Address your letter to the Servicing Manager.

ASSIGNMENT 21

With notebook and pencil at hand, watch a TV programme of your choice.

Write in your book:

a   The name of the programme.

b   The channel and time of transmission.

c   Describe the programme.

d   Say why you chose this programme rather than any other available at the time.

ASSIGNMENT 22

Undertake a small piece of Library Research.

Find out all you can about television.

Find out how programmes are made.

Find out who invented the television.

Word Work

1

Among the words listed below are five which could be used to describe a useful person.

expert   efficient   bungling   ignorant
clumsy   awkward   capable   competent
lazy   slovenly   indolent   proficient

Use a dictionary, if necessary, to find the five words.

Write twelve sentences
Use one of the above words in each sentence.

2

All the words in the box are linked with the idea of SOUND.

humming
squeak
barking
report
screech
clap
rattle
blare

Choose the most suitable word to complete the following sentences.

1 We were alarmed at the ...... of the brakes.
2 I could hear the ...... of cups and saucers.
3 From the cupboard came the faint ...... of a mouse.
4 The loud ...... of thunder could be heard in the mountains.
5 The ...... of bees could be heard in the garden.
6 We awoke to hear the dog ......
7 Margaret said she heard the ...... of a rifle.
8 The ...... of the Hi-Fi was almost deafening.

3

Divide the following list of words into two groups: one group headed COSMETICS the other JEWELLERY.

bangle   aftershave   rouge   powder   lipstick
pendant   necklace   ring   brooch   nail-varnish
shampoo   earring   bracelet   clasp   eye-shadow
perfume   scent   cream   lacquer   deodorant

4

Words which begin with the prefix BI are linked with the idea of two. A BICYCLE is á vehicle with two wheels.
Use your dictionary to find the meaning of these words:

biannual   binocular   bicycle   bilateral   bimetalic   bilingual

Write six sentences using one of the above words in each sentence.

18

PUZZLE PAGE

Obtain a copy of this word grid from your teacher.
Can you fit these words into it?
(Headway English Copymasters 5, number 5. Extra puzzle number 6)

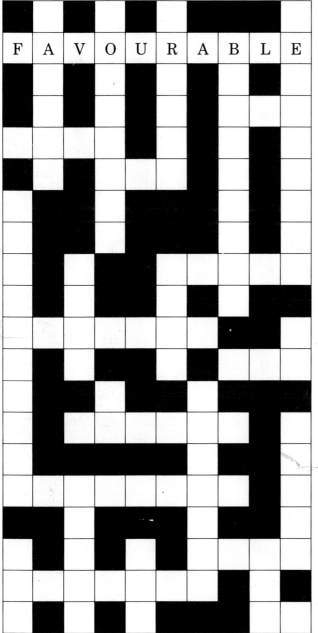

F A V O U R A B L E

Fit these words into the grid at the side of the page.

10 LETTER WORDS

favourable
individual

9 LETTER WORDS

bystander
celebrate

8 LETTER WORDS

romantic
lifebuoy

7 LETTER WORDS

volcano
rejoice
picture

6 LETTER WORDS

Greece
napkin
angler

5 LETTER WORDS

farce
canoe
Crete

4 LETTER WORDS

came   cone
colt   lion

3 LETTER WORDS

pub   man   see
ape   two   tie

2 LETTER WORDS

to   no   an

WHO'S FOR ELEPHANT STEW?

'One man's meat is another man's poison', is an old saying. It suggests that a dish liked by one person would be hated by another. Boiled sheep's eyes, a dish favoured by Arab desert dwellers, would not be generally liked in Britain.

National and regional dishes are indicators of differing taste. The Scots eat haggis. This is a kind of pudding made by boiling offal (the intestines of a pig) in a sheep's stomach. Laverbread is a Welsh delicacy. It is made by boiling seaweed until it turns into a black sticky pulp. It is then eaten fried with bacon and eggs.

In France frogs' legs, snails and horsemeat have for many years been part of the diet. The brightly painted head of a child's rocking horse, fastened over the door of a butcher's shop, is the traditional sign that the butcher sells horsemeat.

Locusts make a good 'starter' to a meal. They taste like shrimp. Chopped elephant tusk boiled with fresh vegetables make excellent stew. For a really tasty meal, the roast hump of a young camel is highly recommended.

All this goes to prove that one man's meat is really another's poison.

Read about the different foods people eat then answer the questions.

1   Who enjoy eating boiled sheep's eyes?

2   Which insect is said to taste like shrimp?

3   Find words in the passage which mean:
    a   a special kind of food.
    b   a dry arid area
    c   not the same as
    d   eaten regularly

4   Name a Welsh, a Scottish and a French delicacy.

5   What is haggis?

6   What is the traditional sign of the horse butcher?

7   Find three methods of cooking
    mentioned in the passage.

8   Teacake is a compound noun.
    It is made up of the words TEA and CAKE.
    Find three other compound nouns in the passage
    which are names of foods.

9   The word 'seasonal' is an adjective.
    It is formed from the word 'season'.
    Find three other adjectives
    which have been formed in the same way.

10 'One man's meat is another man's poison'.
    This is a well known saying.
    Complete these sayings:
    a   Look before you ....
    b   A watched pot never ....
    c   Every cloud has a ....
    d   Too many cooks spoil ....

Word Work

1

Words which begin with the prefix TRI are linked with the idea of Three.

A TRIANGLE is a three sided shape.

Use your dictionary to find the meaning of these words:
trio   triplets   triplicate   tricycle   triennial   tripod

Write six sentences
Use one of the words in each sentence.

triplicate *triplicate* *triplicate*

2

Copy these sentences into your notebook.
Change the words underlined in each sentence
for one of the adverbs taken from the box.

noisily
correctly
carefully
silently
carelessly
bitterly
incorrectly

1 Charles did his maths *in the wrong way*.
2 Margaret did her maths *in the right way*.
3 The nurse bandaged the wound *with great care*.
4 The snow began to fall *without making a sound*.
5 The workmen found it *very* cold while waiting for the bus.
6 The youths ran *with great noise* across the square.

3

Some prefixes when added to a word, change its
meaning, e.g. the prefix 'un', added to 'truth' makes
'untruth'.

Use one of these prefixes:
UN   IM   IN   ILL   DIS
to change the meaning of these words:

honest   able   accurate   visible   usual   fair
true   possible   ability   legal   pure   suitable

Write six sentences.
Use one of the words in each sentence.

4

Copy these sentences into your book.
Choose the most suitable word from those inside the brackets.

1 I (past   passed) my sister on the way to work.

2 He is still (lying   laid   laying) on the grass.

3 The news of the discovery had the (effect   affect) of (raising   rising) the people's hopes.

4 Since you refuse to (accept   except) my (advice   advise) it is (quite   quiet) useless for me to say anything in the (further   future).

5 Each of us (was   were) given a new book by the teacher.

6 None of the men (has   have) worked overtime this week.

7 Neither the train driver nor the guard (was   were) responsible for the accident.

8 A new supermarket (was   were   is) opening in the High Street.

5

Which number is suggested by each of these words?
Write the word and the number in your book.

individual	octave	duplicate	partner	score
none	century	dozen	triangle	hexagon
decimal	triplicate	pair	kilo	half-dozen

6

Replace each of the verbs in these sentences with one of opposite meaning.

1 Harry DESCENDED the rocky path.

2 The government has DECREASED the pension allowance.

3 David has SHORTENED his jeans.

4 Jamie forgot to LOCK the door.

5 The seamen RAISED the ship's gangplank.

Reading for Meaning

EATING IN A RESTAURANT

There are two kinds of restaurant:

SELF-SERVICE

This is for people in a hurry.
The customers select what they want,
pay for it at a cash desk
and carry it away to a table.

WAITER/WAITRESS SERVICE

This is for people who wish to take longer over their meal.
Customers sit at a table, where they select
what they wish to eat from a printed list.
The food is brought to the table
and paid for at the end of the meal.

THE MENU

The list of items on sale is called the MENU.

Many restaurants divide the menu into two parts.

First there is the Meal of the Day.
This is sometimes called the 'table d'hôte' menu.
It is a fixed price meal,
with only a small choice of dishes.

Then there is usually a longer list of dishes available.
This is sometimes called the 'à la carte' menu.

Most restaurants are licensed. This means they serve
alcoholic drinks such as beers, wines and spirits.

Wine is usually sold by the glass, by the carafe
or by the bottle.
A carafe is a type of glass bottle.
It holds a litre of wine.

MENU

Table d'hôte

Soup of the Day
or
Fruit Juice

 . . .

Roast Chicken
Roast Lamb
Grilled Plaice

  . . .

Fruit Salad
or
Ice cream

£4.50.

Coffee Extra

MENU

A La Carte

Starters
Prawn Cocktail ...£1.25
Soup of the Day 60p
Melon (in season) 80p
Fruit Juice 40p
Pâté 60p

Main Course

Roast Chicken £2.40
Roast Duck £4.00
Roast Lamb £3.20
Grilled Ham £1.75
Grilled Plaice £2.50

Sweets

Fruit Salad 75p
Fresh Cream Gateaux
.......................90p
Meringue 60p
Cheese & Biscuits 80p
Ice Cream 40p

Wines & Beer

Lager £1.50
Beer £1.25
House Wine
½ carafe £1.75
carafe £3.00
glass 80p

 VAT Incl.
Gratuities
at the discretion of
the customer.

Answer these questions.

1   Where would you expect to find a self-service restaurant?

2   What is the main difference between a self-service and a waiter-service restaurant?

3   What is a menu?

4   What is a 'table d'hôte' meal?

5   What is an 'à la carte' meal?

6   Find out the meaning of:

Soup of the Day
VAT
Gratuities
in season

7   Choose an 'a la carte' meal which you could buy if you had £7.

8   What is the main difference between the 'table d'hôte'. and the 'à la carte' menus?

ASSIGNMENT 36

Make a list of six different restaurants in your town.

Write in your book:
The name of the restaurant
The address
The telephone number

Use your local telephone directory to find the information.

ASSIGNMENT 37

Describe any restaurant you may have visited.
Describe the place and what you ate.

THE LIMERICK

A limerick is a short, funny poem of only one verse.
Limericks have a set rhyming pattern.
The first two lines rhyme with each other.
Lines three and four rhyme and the final line rhymes with the first.
Here are some examples of limericks.
Each one is on the subject of food and drink.

There was an old man of the coast,
Who quietly sat on a post,
But when it was cold,
He let go his hold,
And called for some hot buttered toast.

There was an old man of Madrid,
Who ate sixty-five eggs for a quid,
When they asked, 'Are you faint?'
He replied, 'No, I ain't,
But I don't feel as well as I did.

There was a young lady of Ryde,
Who ate a green apple and died.
The apple fermented,
Inside the lamented,
And made cider, inside her inside.

A cannibal chief of Penzance,
Ate an uncle and two of his aunts,
And then a large piece
Of a rather fat niece,
And now he can't button his pants.

Put the heading LIMERICKS in your poetry book.
First write a few notes about limericks.
Say what they are. Describe the rhyme pattern.

Copy into your book two of the limericks.
Draw pictures to illustrate the ones you have chosen.

Look in poetry books to find other limericks.
Write some of the ones you like in your book.

With a partner, see if you can write a limerick.
Collect together all the limericks written by your class
into an anthology.

PUZZLE PAGE

ASSIGNMENT 39

Obtain a copy of this puzzle from your teacher.
(Headway English Copymasters 5, number 7.
Extra puzzle numbers 8 and 9.)

Fit the words listed below into the puzzle.

Fit the words clockwise, so that the last two letters
of one word become the first two letters of the next.

alternate	amateur	catarrh	ceased	chinese
educates	engrave	emotion	empty	esteem
ethnic	gem	ice-cream	idle	language
leanest	lymphatic	onset	orderly	ostrich
reduce	rhinoceros	several	stamen	temperature
typhoid	umbrella	uranium	vendor	

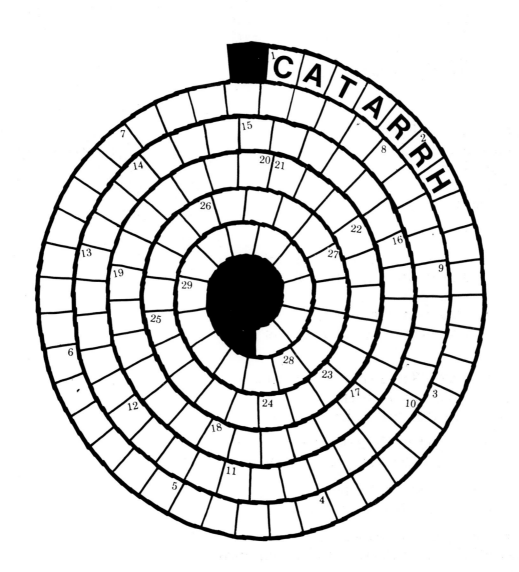

27

When the year will have an extra day

A year is made up of three-hundred-and-sixty-five days. This is called a 'calendar year.' Another kind of year is the solar year. This is the time it takes for planet Earth to move once around the Sun. The solar year is just under six hours longer than the calendar year. Because of this difference, it is necessary to add an extra day to the calendar year every four years. When this happens it is called a leap year. The extra day is always added to February, making twenty-nine days instead of the usual twenty-eight. However, even this adjustment is not sufficient to make both the calendar and the solar years coincide. Once every four hundred years yet another extra day must be added to the calendar year. The next time this happens will be the year 2000.

Our present calendar began in 1582 on the orders of Pope Gregory. It is called the Gregorian calendar. Before Pope Gregory introduced his calendar people lived according to a calendar begun in Roman times. This calendar divided the year into periods of ten months. In this calendar, October was the eighth month and December the tenth.

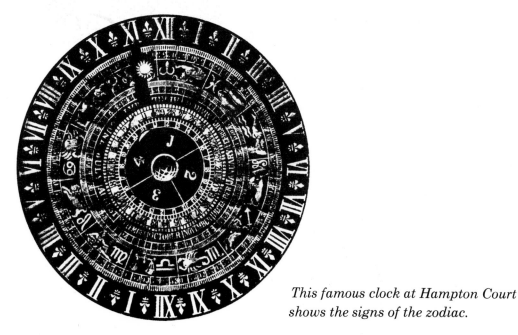

This famous clock at Hampton Court shows the signs of the zodiac.

Calendar 1987

January February March

April May June

July August September

October November December

Religious Festivals in 1987

Christian — Western

Ash Wednesday	March
Quadragesima	March
Palm Sunday	April
Good Friday	April
Easter Day	April
Ascension Day	May
Whit Sunday	June
Trinity Sunday	June
Corpus Christi	June
Advent Sunday	November
Christmas	December

Christian — Eastern Orthodox

Lent Monday	March
Easter Day	April
Pentecost	June

Christian — Coptic

Easter Day	April

Chinese

Lunar New Year (3 days)	January 29 -

Hindu Dates not available at time of going to press

Islamic (dates subject to visibility of new moon)

Laylat-ul-Mi'raj	March
1st of Ramadan	April
Id-al-Fitr	May
Id-al-Adha	August
Al-Hijra (Islamic New Year) AH 1408	August
Ashura	September
Milad-al-Nabi	November

Jewish

Pessach (Passover)	April
Shavuot (Pentecost)	June
Fast of 17 Tammuz	July
Fast of 9 Ab	August
Rosh Hashanah (Jewish New Year) AM 5748	September
Yom Kippur (Day of Atonement)	October
Succot (Tabernacles)	October
Chanukah	December

Sikh

Birthday of Guru Gobind Singh Ji	January 6, December
Baisakhi	April
Martyrdom of Guru Arjan Dev Ji	May
Birthday of Guru Nanak Dev Ji	November
Martyrdom of Guru Teg Bahadur	November

Calendar 1988

January February March

April May June

July August September

October November December

Read the passage about the Calendar, then answer these questions.

1 What is meant by the phrases:
   a the solar year
   b the calendar year

2 Is the calendar year
   a longer
   b shorter
   c the same as the solar year
   What is the difference in time, if any?

3 What is a leap year?
   What difference is made to our calendar during this year?

4 What change will take place in the calendar during the year 2000?
   When did this change last take place?

5 When did our present calendar begin?
   Who began it?

6 In the Roman calendar, October was the eighth month and December the tenth.
   What is the position of October and December in our calendar?

7 In the passage, Earth is called a planet.
   Name three other planets.

8 On many calendars, certain days are marked as a Bank Holiday?
   What is a Bank Holiday?
   When do they occur?

9 Some days are marked on the calendar as Saints' Days.
   Find out the dates of some of these.

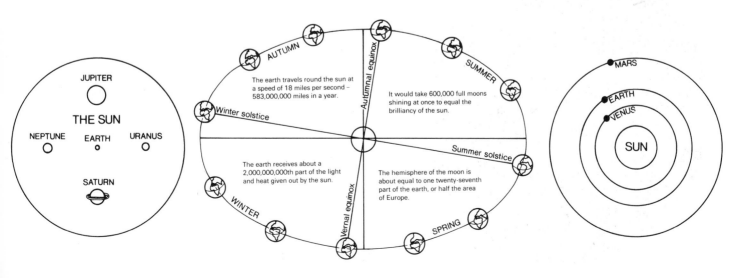

JUPITER

THE SUN

NEPTUNE   EARTH   URANUS

SATURN

AUTUMN

Autumnal equinox

SUMMER

The earth travels round the sun at a speed of 18 miles per second – 583,000,000 miles in a year.

It would take 600,000 full moons shining at once to equal the brilliancy of the sun.

Winter solstice

Summer solstice

The earth receives about a 2,000,000,000th part of the light and heat given out by the sun.

The hemisphere of the moon is about equal to one twenty-seventh part of the earth, or half the area of Europe.

WINTER

Vernal equinox

SPRING

MARS

EARTH

VENUS

SUN

Word Work

1

Complete the sentences by choosing one word taken from those
in the brackets.
Use a dictionary if necessary.

Gigantic is similar to .... (small   huge   mean)
Extravagant is similar to .... (hopeful   wasteful   lavish)
Economical is similar to .... (sparing   wasteful   generous)
Impudent is similar to .... (cheeky   polite   rowdy)
Obstinate is similar to .... (boring   stubborn   rude)
Vaguely is similar to .... (dimly   quickly   patiently)

Write six sentences. Use one of the words in each sentence.

2

What do we call each of these?
Match each of these words with their meaning:

illustrations   garage   crypt   link
heirloom   attic   office   genius

1   the basement of a church
2   a small room at the top of a house
3   any item handed down from one
    generation to the next
4   a room where clerks and typists work
5   pictures and drawings in a book
6   someone of very great ability
7   a place where cars are kept
8   part of a chain

3

Divide the words printed below into two groups
words linked with the idea of **HEAT** and words linked with the idea of **COLD**:

tropical   frosty   freezing   polar   frozen   chilly
stifling   fiery   wintry   arctic   stuffy   close
equatorial   humid   sizzling   antarctic   icy

4

Answer these questions.
To find the answer you will probably need to look up the underlined word in your dictionary.

1 What is missing from an *anonymous* letter?
2 Name any *accessory* which goes with a camera.
3 Is an orange a *succulent* fruit?
4 What kind of *tournament* is held at Wimbledon?
5 Is smoking an *innocuous* habit?
6 Is a *skirmish* a big battle?
7 Would you feel squashed in a *spacious* room?
8 If the voting in an election is *unanimous*
   does this mean there is total agreement
   among the voters?
9 Would you be able to drive a car down a *barricaded* street?

5

Here are a number of expressions used in everyday speech.
Their meaning would be very confusing to a foreign visitor.

1   At sixes and sevens
2   The apple of one's eye
3   A wet blanket
4   The man in the street
5   At the eleventh hour
6   At loggerheads
7   Lionhearted
8   Stuck-up
9   A peppery individual
10 Heavy-eyed

Here are the meanings of each of them.

Match each of the expressions with its meaning.

a   someone who is bad tempered
b   to be all mixed up
c   to be conceited
d   to have great courage
e   to be specially loved
f   to be discouraging
g   at the last minute
h   to be half asleep
i   an ordinary person
j   to be always quarrelling

Kinds of Poetry

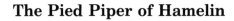

THE BALLAD

In the days of the Normans, a frequent visitor to the castles was the minstrel. The minstrel told stories in the form of songs. They were usually about love and the deeds of brave knights. These anonymous minstrel stories are known as ballads.

Eventually, the ballads were written down and, with the discovery of printing, they became widely known. Poets started to make these old stories into poems. These poems often have a sing-song rhythm and sometimes one or two lines are repeated at the end of every verse, like the chorus of a song.

The Pied Piper of Hamelin

According to legend, the German town of Hamelin was infested by rats. One day, a man dressed in a multi-coloured suit, offered to rid the town of the vermin, for a payment of a thousand gold coins.

The town council agreed and as promised the piper got rid of the rats. They were attracted by his pipe playing. They followed him and he led them to the river, where they all tumbled in and were drowned. When he returned to claim his payment, the mayor refused to pay.

Taking vengeance, the piper again walked the streets playing his pipe. This time it was the children who followed the mysterious man. He led them away. They were never seen again.

Here is the opening of the poet Browning's famous ballad.

Hamelin Town's in Brunswick,
By famous Hanover city;
The river Weser, deep and wide,
Washes its wall on the southern side;
A pleasanter spot you never spied;
But, when begins my ditty,
Almost five hundred years ago,
To see the townsfolk suffer so
From vermin was a pity.

Rats!
They fought the dogs, and killed the cats,
And bit the babies in the cradles,
And ate the cheeses out of the vats,
And licked the soup from the cooks' own ladles,
Split open the kegs of salted sprats,
Made nests inside men's Sunday hats,
And even spoiled the women's chats,
By drowning their speaking
With shrieking and squeaking
In fifty different sharps and flats.

THINGS TO DO

What is a ballad poem?
Copy the beginning of the Pied Piper poem into your book.
Write the story of the Pied Piper as if your were
the Piper himself, the mayor or one of the parents.

Browning wrote the poem to amuse a small boy and
sent it to him with the suggestion that he might draw
illustrations for it.
Look at pictures of German towns in order to get an idea
of what they look like.
Now draw your own illustration for the poem.

ASSIGNMENT 47

Read the story of Robin Hood.
If possible read the story of what happened
when Robin met the Bishop of Hereford.
Tell the story in your own words as if you were the Bishop,
Robin Hood or one of his men.

Writing Work

1 Write a description of any building in your town.
If possible find out the history of the building.
Describe what activities go on in it.

2 Visit your grandparents or any other old person
who you may know.

Ask them questions about their schooldays.
Ask them about the places in which they worked.
Ask them about the clothes they wore.
Ask them about their leisure activities.

First make a list of the questions you will ask.
Make notes while you are with the person.
If possible, tape-record your visit.
Now write up your interview.

3 Here are pictures of four famous buildings.
Use reference books and encyclopaedias to find out
all you can about them.
Draw pictures of the buildings.
Write eight sentences about any three of them.

4 Copy these sayings into your book.
Write a phrase or short sentence to explain each one:

a to take heart
b to take to heart
c to one's heart's content
d to know by heart

e the heart of the matter
f to have a heavy heart
g to break one's heart
h to lose one's heart

Write eight sentences
Use one of the expressions in each sentence.

PUZZLE PAGE

SIMILES

Similes are short comparative statements.

e.g. as cunning as a fox.

Obtain a copy of this puzzle (Headway Copymasters 5, number 10.

Extra puzzles numbers 11 and 12).

Find the word which completes each of these similes.

Do so by rearranging the letters found in the second box.

1	as blind as a	A B T
2	as fat as a	G P I
3	as fierce as a	N L O I
4	as graceful as a	S N W A
5	as gentle as a	D E O V
6	as hungry as a	O L F W
7	as obstinate as a ..	L M U E
8	as patient as	B J O
9	as pleased as	H C N U P
10	as quiet as a	U M O S E
11	as tall as a	T A G I N
12	as wise an an	O M S O L O N
13	as white as a	O G H S T
14	as black as	C O A L
15	as bold as	S A B R S
16	as dead as	N I G T H
17	as hot as a	F A U R C N E
18	as tough as	T H L E A E R
19	as easy as	W N G I N K I
20	as deaf as a	T P S O

Scotland's most romantic village
GRETNA GREEN

There are few places in Scotland which conjure up the idea of romance better than Gretna Green. Gretna is a small village. It stands a few hundred yards over the border which separates England from Scotland.

Gretna's fame began in 1754 when a law was passed which made instant marriages impossible in England. In Scotland, however, it remained possible for a couple to simply declare before a witness that from now on they intended to live together as man and wife. No priest was needed and no waiting period was necessary.

Thousands of couples from England who wanted a quick wedding soon began to flock to the forge at Gretna. Most of them were running away from the fury of their parents who did not approve of the marriage. They stood beside the anvil and, for a small fee, the blacksmith was willing to be a witness to their wedding.

Today, Gretna Green is a tourist centre. Visitors mainly come to see the old blacksmith's forge and his famous anvil. They also come to the village to buy woollen kilts and jumpers made by weavers whose work is renowned.

Gretna Hall,
the original Marriage House.

Read about Scotland's most romantic village, Gretna Green, then answer these questions.

1   When were the marriage laws of England changed so as to make marriages more difficult?

2   Why did young couples cross the border into Scotland to marry?

3   Which of these words means 'running away to get married': elapsing, eloping or eliciting?

4   What tourist attractions are there at Gretna Green today?
    Name the article of clothing mentioned which is usually associated with Scotland.

5   The Gretna blacksmith used an anvil while he worked at the forge.
    Sort these lists into occupation, tools used and places of work:

building site	scalpel	teacher
hospital	blackboard	gardener
greenhouse	hoe	bricklayer
school	trowel	surgeon

6   Find words in the passage which mean:

    payment   clergyman   immediate   anger   famous

7   Arrange the items in each of these lists in order of size, largest first:

    city   village   hamlet   town
    hundred   couple   few   thousands   dozen
    universe   world   country   continent

8   Which of these statements is true?
    Copy the statement into your book.
    Write the word **TRUE** or **FALSE**
    at the end of each one.

    a   Gretna Green is a small Yorkshire village.
    b   To-day's visitors can buy woollen kilts at Gretna.
    c   Couples were once married at Gretna by the village carpenter.

Word Work

1 Arrange the following words into two groups.

words which suggest **SIMILARITY:**
words which suggest **DISSIMILARITY:**

resemblance	unlike	congruity	different
likeness	diverse	parity	incompatible
discordant	odd	reflection	unrelated
distinct	twin	equal	equivalent

Write six sentences
Use any one of the words in each sentence.

---

2 For each of the words printed below choose the best meaning from the three given.
Write the word and its meaning in your book.

PENALTY
a gain
b rule
c punishment

BLEACH
a rip apart
b whiten
c destroy

NORMAL
a insane
b funny
c usual

CAREFREE
a without authority
b without worry
c honesty

COMBINE
a to talk about
b to join together
c to separate

FURIOUS
a careless
b angry
c sad

PLEDGE
a promise
b request
c faith

CONSULT
a behave well
b to eat up
c to seek advice

IDENTIFY
a try harder
b to guess
c to recognise

ANXIOUS
a inactive
b unsure
c worried

DRAMATISE
a to think about
b to act out
c to change over

PARALYSE
a act slowly
b make powerless
c to speed up

---

3 Add a prefix to each of these words
in order to give them their opposite meaning:

possible	behave	please	perfect	trust
reasonable	responsible	complete	observed	agree

Write ten sentences.
Use one of the words you have made in each sentence.

4

These pairs of words are often confused:

accept/except   amiable/amicable
advise/advice   arms/alms
aid/aide   ascent/assent
allay/ally   averse/adverse
allude/elude   ajoin/adjourn

**Use your dictionary to find the meaning
of each word.**
Choose any eight of them.
Write sentences to show how each of the words
can be used.

5

A proverb is a short, familiar saying
expressing a well-known truth or wise thought.
Arrange the following proverbs in pairs
so that the first proverb in each pair
seems to contradict the other.

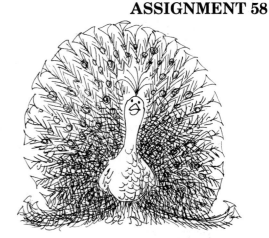

1   Absence makes the heart grow fonder.
2   Fine feathers make fine birds.
3   A miss is as good as a mile.
4   Don't judge the marmalade by its label.
5   Out of sight out of mind.
6   Too many cooks spoil the broth.
7   Better late than never.
8   He who hesitates is lost.
9   Look before you leap.
10   Many hands make light work.

Choose any five of the proverbs.
Write sentences to explain their meaning.

LIFE SKILLS

WHAT HAPPENS WHEN I LEAVE?

Just before you leave school you will be interviewed
by someone from the **CAREERS OFFICE**.
The Careers Officer knows about both job vacancies
and training opportunities in your area.
Whether you go straight from school to a training
course or into a job, one of the first things you will be
asked to do is fill in one of the career's office forms.
Before going to the interview and before filling in the form,
you will have to consider the type of work
you would like to do.
In addition to the reward of money,
there are other satisfactions to be gained
from working and training.
These are some of them:

> job security
> regular hours
> friendly workmates
> chance of promotion
> good working environment
> training opportunity
> plenty of variety
> good canteen facilities
> lots of overtime
> chance of travel
> meeting people
> job satisfaction

ASSIGNMENT 59

Rewrite the above list in the order you consider
to be the most important.

Find out the following details about your local Careers Office:

address   opening hours   telephone number

FORM FILLING

Obtain a copy of these forms from your teacher.
(Headway English Copymasters 5, numbers 13 and 14).
Complete each of the forms.
Remember you will want to make a good impression.
Fill in the forms neatly.
Check your spelling.
Use a dictionary if you are not sure.

KINGTOWN COUNTY COUNCIL   **Careers Office**

Surname .... First name ....
Date of birth .... School leaving date ....
Name of school .... Class ......
What school subjects do you like most? ....
....
Which are you best at? ....
What school subjects do you like least? ....
....
Which sports do you play? ....
....

Would you like to continue your education full-time? ....
At school? ....   At a technical college? ....
Have you any special interests (e.g. sports, clubs, hobbies?) ....
Please list them ....
....
....

Have you made any enquiries about work yourself? ....
If so, please give full details ....
....
....
Do you know of any place where you would particularly like to work?
If so, please give details here
....
....
....
Would you work and live away from home if necessary? ....

LIFE SKILLS

KINGTOWN COUNTY COUNCIL   **Careers Office**

Here are some working situations in which you could find yourself. If there are any that you do NOT like, cross them out:

in an office	with your hands	with or for people
in engineering	with figures	in a laboratory
outside all the time	further study	selling things

Here are four lists of jobs.
Underline three you think you would like:

Words/Figures	**Practical**	**Active**	**People**
Filing clerk	Cook	Building worker	Hotel porter
Storeman	Garage mechanic	Miner	Railway porter
Cashier	Gardener	Quarryman	Waiter/Waitress
Meter reader	Farm worker	Postman	Sales assistant
Delivery man	Factory worker	Ambulance driver	Hospital worker
Telephonist	Painter	Fireman	Bus conductor
Typist	Dressmaker	Van driver	Receptionist
General clerk	Bricklayer	Domestic worker	
	Plumber	Shelf filler	
	Panel beater	Bus driver	
	Hair stylist		

Now look at the three jobs you have underlined.
Put (1) in front of the job you would like best, put (2) and (3) in front of the others according to preference.

State any job not listed above you would like ....
Put a cross (X) opposite any job you would definitely dislike and give reasons below:

....

....

Are there any special reasons (physical or medical) why you should not take up any particular occupation? If so, please give brief details:

....

....

Give briefly any other points you, or your parents, think are important to both your career and future:

....

....

ASSIGNMENT 61

Here are the names of six jobs:

HAIR STYLIST	**TRANSPORT WORKER**
FARM WORKER	**POLICE OFFICER**
CHEF-COOK	**SHOP WORKER**

If you were offered one of these jobs, make a list of the things you think you would like about the job.

PUZZLE PAGE

Obtain a copy of this puzzle from your teacher.
(Headway English Copymasters 5, number 15).
Within the puzzle are the names of several different kinds of jobs.
Find each job name. Write each name in your notebook.

Ambulance crew	Driver	Hairstylist	Panelbeater	Telephonist
Builder	Dressmaker	Mechanic	Postman	Typist
Clerk	Fitter	Machinist	Glazier	Shelf-filler
Cashier	Farmworker	Miner	Painter	Vanman
Cook	Fireman	Nurse	Storeman	Waiter
	Gardener	Plumber	Salesman	Porter

A	G	A	R	D	E	N	E	R	Z	O	O	K	T	S	R
D	M	E	C	H	A	N	I	C	T	R	I	T	E	H	E
R	A	B	P	A	I	N	T	E	R	E	P	S	L	E	T
E	Q	V	U	C	L	A	R	O	S	I	J	I	E	L	R
S	T	B	C	L	A	V	C	R	S	M	N	L	P	F	O
S	F	V	R	E	A	O	S	T	P	R	I	Y	H	F	P
M	I	N	E	R	O	N	Z	I	E	J	K	T	O	I	P
A	R	D	D	K	E	G	C	I	L	H	D	S	N	L	R
K	E	Q	L	O	V	L	Z	E	A	U	R	R	I	L	S
E	M	R	I	S	M	A	T	U	C	B	I	I	S	E	Z
R	A	N	U	P	L	U	M	B	E	R	V	A	T	R	N
V	N	J	B	G	R	E	T	I	A	W	E	H	S	M	A
F	A	R	M	W	O	R	K	E	R	J	R	W	X	T	M
I	S	N	M	U	X	V	L	N	A	M	E	R	O	T	S
T	R	M	M	A	C	H	I	N	I	S	T	T	V	A	E
T	S	O	C	A	S	H	I	E	R	L	V	W	K	M	L
E	Z	Q	P	F	N	J	L	N	A	M	T	S	O	P	A
R	P	A	N	E	L	B	E	A	T	E	R	M	J	B	S

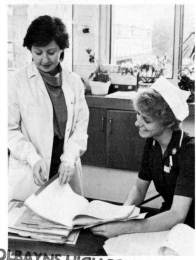

COLBAYNS HIGH SCHOOL
Clacton-on-Sea. CO15 3JL

TOMBS OF THE PHAROAHS

Two thousand years ago, a Greek writer made a list of what he thought were the Wonders of the World. He listed seven. Included in this list were The Pyramids – the three great royal tombs which stand near the river Nile at Cairo, Egypt's capital.

The biggest of the three tombs is the burial place of Pharaoh Cheops. Pharaoh is the old Egyptian name for a king. The tomb of Cheops was one of the biggest buildings in the world at the time it was built, and is four-hundred-and-fifty feet high. Nearly two million huge blocks of stone were needed to make it.

The tomb was built just over four thousand years ago. Deep inside is the burial room. It was in this room that the body of Pharaoh Cheops, was laid in a golden coffin. Great piles of treasures were placed in an adjoining room. It was thought the king would need this in his next life. The tomb was then sealed for hundreds of years until it was attacked by robbers.

Visitors to modern Cairo are often surprised to find that there are other pyramids. A few miles along the river is the Step Pyramid, one of the world's oldest buildings. This is a thousand years older than its more famous neighbours. It is called the 'Step Pyramid' because it rises in a series of steep steps from the base to the apex.

Read about the Pyramids of Egypt then answer the
questions.

1 Who wrote about the Wonders of the World?
How many were there?

2 What are The Pyramids?
Where can they be seen?
How many of them are there?

3 Who is buried in the biggest of the Cairo pyramids?

4 How high is Cheops' tomb.
How many stone blocks
were used in its construction?

5 When was the tomb built?
Describe Cheop's coffin.
What else was buried with the body?

6 Are the Cairo pyramids the only ones in Egypt?
Write three sentences about another pyramid
described in the passage.

7 Change one word in each of these sentences
to make them correct.
a The Step pyramid is a thousand years
younger than those in Cairo.
b A Roman writer listed the Seven Wonders
of the World.
c Pharaoh Cheops was buried in a silver coffin.

8 Egyptians come from Egypt.
What is the name given to the people of:
Germany Bulgaria France Switzerland
Holland Greece Spain China Thailand

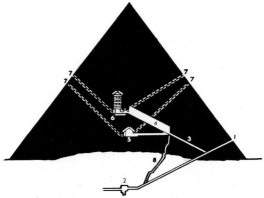

1 Entrance on the north face of the pyramid
2 Unfinished chamber; in many other pyramids this is where
the burial chamber was
3 Passage leading to the 'Grand Gallery'
4 'Grand Gallery', guarded by heavy stone portcullises
5 'Queen's Chamber'
6 'King's Chamber' — at the west end of this is the sarco-
phagus of Cheops
7 Ventilating Shafts
8 Well shaft

Word Work

1

Choose the best definition for each of the words printed below. Write the word and its meaning in your book.

IDOLISE
a brighten up
b greatly admire
c decorate

DISCORD
a obedient
b without harmony
c unreasonable

CHASTE
a hurried
b pure
c willing

DORMANT
a inactive
b stale
c separate

NOMAD
a dwarf
b gypsy
c wanderer

DECREPIT
a old and feeble
b new and shiny
c cold and wet

HARROWING
a weakening
b disturbing
c sickening

PRELUDE
a an explanation
b a sign
c an introduction

CLARIFY
a explain
b disprove
c solve

SLOVENLY
a be untidy
b bad tempered
c disobedient

TURBULENT
a nervous
b violent
c dramatic

COAX
a bury
b persuade
c punish

2

Look at these words:

novel	dictionary	time-table	catalogue
telephone directory	album	scrapbook	log
diary	calendar	atlas	register

All the above words are the names of different kinds of books.

Which of the above books would you look in to find:

a record of a person's daily thoughts and activities
b the day and date of the month
c the position of a place or country
d the time of a train or bus
e record of attendance at school
f a fictitious tale
g details of a ship's voyage
h a collection of photographs
i the meaning of a word
j details of things for sale
k a telephone number
l newspaper cuttings

AUCTION SALE CATALOGUE

OF

FURNITURE & EFFECTS

ON

WEDNESDAY, 13th MAY 1987 at 10 a.m.

1 2 China Meat Dishes, a Denby ware Hot Water Jug a a Beer Tankard.
2 A quantity of Pottery, Jardinieres, Vases, etc.
3 2 Chromium plated Thermos Flasks.
4 A stainless steel Ice Bucket and Sparklets Soda Sy,
5 A quantity of Royal Doulton Burgundy pattern china 19 pieces.
6 A quantity of leaf pattern modern china Dinner ware 36 pieces.
7 2 Pairs of double bracket modern Wall Lights with o, glass shades.
8 — ditto —
9 A single double Wall Light brac
10 A quantity of embr

3

Copy these sentences into your notebook.
Change the words in italics in each sentence for one
of the words taken from the box.

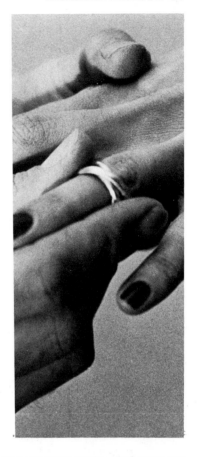

eluded
callous
amiable
breached
consented
biannual

1 The thief *slipped away from* her captors.
2 Judi was described by her workmates
   as a *friendly, good natured* person.
3 Arjun's parents gave
   their notice that they were willing
   for him to marry Wendy.
4 On Thursday evening,
   Neil went to the *twice yearly* meeting
   of the fishing club.
5 The thieves *got through* the wall
   dividing the café from the bank.
6 Angela was thought of as a *hard,
   unfeeling* person.

4

All the sentences contain common mistakes.
Copy and correct them.
1 I didn't now as you were coming.
2 It was him who done it.
3 He is much more clever than me.
4 I saw the man which you described.
5 Keeping a dog tied up can make them go mad.
6 Why wasn't you at school, yesterday?
7 I hope you will allow I and he to go.
8 I said to the porter, 'Which is my cases?'

5

Add a prefix to each of these words to make a word
of opposite meaning.

proper	civil	orderly	behave	natural
sense	correct	truthful	honour	capable

Write ten sentences. Use one of the new words in each sentence.

LIFE SKILLS

WHAT NEXT . . . THE YOUTH TRAINING SCHEME

When you become sixteen, you will have to decide
what you wish to do when the time comes
for you to leave school.
Several choices may be open to you. You could:

Stay on at school
Attend a College of Further Education
Get a job
Join one of the many and varied Youth Training Schemes

The Youth Training Scheme, known as YTS, is a
Government scheme set up to provide training for young
people.

Training for a job is an important part of your continuing
education. Being educated does not stop when you leave
school. All the best jobs require a period of training.
This training period can last for several years.

A YTS training scheme lasts for 2 years.
Each week you will work for about 40 hours
at your training programme.
While on your programme you will be paid a training
allowance. If you have to leave home to train, you will be
paid a lodging allowance.
Like other workers you will get 18 days holiday with full
pay and any Bank Holidays which arise during the period
of training.
There is now a YTS scheme for almost any job.

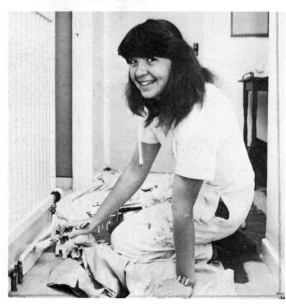

There are YTS schemes suited to the building industry,
hairdressing, working in a shop or office, in agriculture,
in the clothing trade, in hospitals, and children's and old
people's homes.

A YTS scheme is divided into three parts.

PART 1

This is called the Period of Induction and lasts
about a fortnight or three weeks.
During this time you will be shown around the place
where you will be working.
You will be told about safety regulations, discipline
and grievance procedures, hours of work and wages.

PART 2

This part is called the **ON-THE-JOB** training period.
During this period, you will be given the chance to try
several different kinds of job.
Different kinds of work experience may take place
in the same workplace or you may be moved to others.
Wherever you work you will be closely supervised
so that you can get the best training and experience.

PART 3

This is called the **OFF-THE-JOB** training period.
There will be two periods of off-the-job training.
For this you will go either to college or to a special
training centre.
In the first year, there will be a period of thirteen weeks
and in the second year a period of seven.
During this time, you will attend classes to teach you
the theory behind the job you are doing.
There will also be classes to improve your general
education.

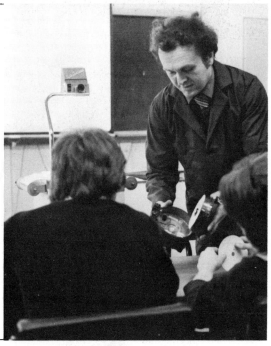

LIFE SKILLS

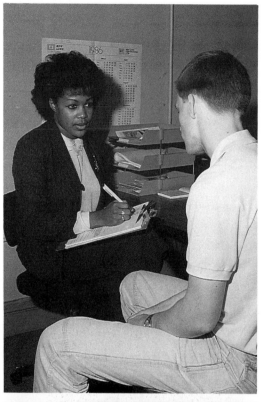

Read about the Youth Training Scheme (YTS)
then answer these questions.

1 What four possibilities are open to young people
when they reach the school leaving age?

2 What does the YTS scheme provide for young
people?

3 What is the normal length of a YTS scheme?

4 If you join a YTS scheme, how many hours each week
will you work at your training?

5 Will you get a training allowance while you are
on a YTS scheme?

6 How much holiday will you be given?

7 If you join a YTS scheme there will be a period
of induction.
What happens during this period?
How long does it last?

8 What do you understand by 'on-the-job training?'

9 Would you expect to be supervised during your
on-the-job training?

10 What is off-the-job training?

11 Does off-the-job training take place at the same
place where you do your on-the-job training?

12 How long does the off-the-job training last?

GETTING MORE INFORMATION

Write a letter to the Manager
of the Youth Training Scheme
for your area.
Request someone to come to your school and talk to you
about the YTS schemes that are going on in your area.
You will find the address in your telephone directory.
Look up **MANPOWER SERVICES COMMISSION,
AREA TRAINING OFFICE.**

PUZZLE PAGE

Ask your teacher for a copy of this puzzle.
(Headway English Copymasters 5, number 16.)
Complete the word puzzle first.
This will help you decode the longer puzzle
at the bottom of the page.

1 This commission organises YTS courses
2 This is needed before starting most jobs
3 Payment for work done
4 365 days make one of these
5 A great land mass
6 Not pretty
7 A colour of the rainbow
8 Cars sometimes do this – especially on icy roads
9 To rush
10 To poke in a rough way

	A	B	C	D	E	F	G	H	I
1	M	A	N	P	O	W	E	R	
2	T	R	A	I	N	I	N	G	
3	W	A	G	E	S				
4			Y	E	A	R			
5	C	O	N	T	I	N	E	N	T
6			U	G	L	Y			
7	V	O	L	E					
8			S	K	I	B			
9		H	U	R	R	Y			
10	J	A	B						

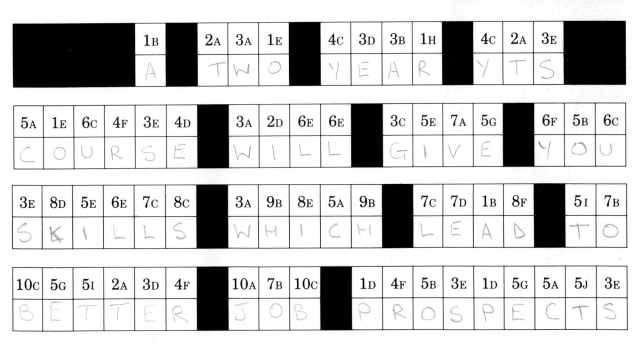

A TWO YEAR YTS

COURSE WILL GIVE YOU

SKILLS WHICH LEAD TO

BETTER JOB PROSPECTS

51

PONY TREKKING

Although it is largely a minority sport, pony trekking continues to grow in popularity. Pony trekking provides an opportunity to explore countryside which, except on foot, would otherwise be inaccessible.

Trekking centres are often found in those parts of the country where the terrain is wild and varied. There are trekking centres in various parts of Scotland, Wales, the Yorkshire Moors and Exmoor.

The cost of staying at a centre includes the hire of a pony. When you arrive at the centre you will be allocated a pony. It is your job, while you are there, to feed, groom and generally look after the animal. Sometimes, it is possible for you to take your own pony to a centre.

Each day, after a large breakfast you will be able to trek across the neighbouring countryside. The centre organiser will have already thought about the length of the trek and the difficulties to be encountered. Where you go will depend on your riding ability and experience. Usually a group of riders go trekking together and this provides an opportunity to make new friends.

Ponies are a breed of small horse. A fully grown pony rarely stands more than two metres high at the shoulders. The main breeds of pony are the Shetland, the Welsh and Hackney. Although Shetland ponies look frail, they are strong animals and, by tradition, were the beast of burden on Shetland, their native island in the north of Scotland.

Read about ponies and pony trekking, then answer the
questions.

1 What are ponies?

2 Name three breeds of pony.

3 Describe a Shetland pony.

4 What type of countryside is usually chosen for a pony trek?

5 Name two areas of Britain where pony trekking centres can be found.

6 Besides trekking, what else would you expect to do on a trekking holiday?

7 Ponies is the plural of pony.
   Write out the plural of the following:
   penny cherry lady pastry

8 Find a word or words in the passage which mean:
   a how skilful you are
   b out of reach
   c chance
   d difficult to reach

9 These words are found in the passage:
   frail native friend minority
   Match each one with its opposite, listed below:
   majority enemy strong foreign

10 Copy into your book only the statements that are true.
    a Shetland ponies are strong animals.
    b A day out pony trekking usually begins with a light breakfast.
    c In order to trek it is necessary to have your own pony.
    d Trekking is a minority sport.
    e Trekking is a good way to make new friends.
    f Trekking centres can be found in various parts of Britain.

Writing Work

APPLYING FOR A JOB

If you need to write a letter applying for a job, this plan will help you.

1 Your address

2 The date

3 Name of person (if known)
4 Position (if known)
5 Address of firm

6 Start with 'Dear Sir' or 'Dear Madam'
7 State the name of the job
8 State where you saw the advert
9 Say something about yourself: age, qualifications, date of leaving school
10 Say you would like to go for an interview.
11 Give the name and address of your referees
12 End with 'Yours faithfully'
Sign your name clearly.

Situations Vacant

VACANCY

Junior storeperson wanted. Some overtime required at weekends. Would suit **school** leaver. Apply in writing with the names of two referees, to **The Personnel Manager, Meadowbank Engineering, Downland Way, Blackwood Gwent, NP2.2AA**

Newspapers often carry advertisements for firms which have job vacancies.
Jobs appear in the column called
SITUATIONS VACANT.
Sometimes a job advert will say
'reply in writing with the names of two referees'.
Referees are people who know you well and who are prepared to write a reference for you.

This is what a reply using the plan would look like.
The job vacancy appeared in the Blackwood Advertiser, on Thursday, June 11th.

Copy the plan of the job application letter into your book.

36, Oak Street
Greenwood Estate
Blackwood
Gwent NP2 2AE.

14th June 1987

The Personnel Manager
Meadowbank Engineering
Downland Way
Blackwood
Gwent

Dear Sir

I would like to apply for the job of Junior Storeperson which was advertised in the Blackwood Advertiser on June 11th.

I am 16 years old and attend Blackwood Comprehensive School. I shall leave on July 4th this year.

My GCSE passes include Maths, English, Workshop Practice and Woodwork.

I would be very pleased to attend an interview. My referees are Mr D. Wilson of John's Garage, Blackwood and Mrs E. Smith, my Form Teacher at Blackwood Comprehensive.

I look forward to hearing from you.

Yours faithfully
Ian Dandy.

This is how Ken Brown replied to the advertisement
for a Junior Storeperson.

> 25 bank st
> blackwood
>
> Personal manager
> meadow Bank engineer
> Blackwood gwent
>
> Dear sir
> I have seen your advert in a paper,
> for a storeman job. I can come and
> see you on wednesday. Mr Jones my
> teacher ~~ant~~ will speak for me,
> yours faithful
> Ken Brown.

Rewrite the letter correctly.
Use the names and addresses of your own referees to
complete the letter.

Before you give the name and address of a person
as your referee, you must ask their permission.
This often means writing to them. When you write
you must send them particulars of the job
you are seeking.
You must also thank the person concerned for doing
you the favour.
Write a letter to one of your referees asking for a reference.

FORM FILLING

Whenever you apply for a job,
you will be asked to fill in an application form.
When filling in forms, take time and care.
First write the answers on a piece of paper.
When you are sure you know the answers,
and the spelling is correct,
then fill in the form.
Obtain a copy of this form from your teacher and complete it.
(Headway English Copymasters 5, number 17).

Greenmeadow Plastics Ltd.
Unity Industrial Estate, Greenmeadow, Kingtonshire
APPLICATION FOR EMPLOYMENT

Surname (block capitals) ....

First name(s) ....

Address ....

Date of birth .... Place of birth ....

Nationality ....

Schools attended in last three years with dates:

....

....

....

Leaving date ....

Examinations taken or to be taken (state GCSE, etc):

....

....

....

If the results are not yet available, state when you expect to receive
them:

....

Hobbies and interests ....

....

Club or society membership ....

....

Games played ....

Has any illness or accident kept you away from school for more than a
week during the last three years?

If so, please give details: ....

....

....

....

State the type of work in which you are interested: ....

....

Signature of applicant .... Date ....

This form is an example of one you will be asked to complete when you are offered a job.
Obtain a copy of the form from your teacher.
(Headway English Copymasters 5, number 18).
Answer the questions.

Greenmeadow Plastics Ltd.
EMPLOYEE'S RECORD CARD

Surname .... First name(s) ....
Address ....
....
....
....
Date of Birth .... Married or single ....
National Insurance Number

☐ ☐ ☐ ☐ ☐ ☐ ☐ ☐ ☐

Name of Doctor ....
Surgery address ....
Address ....
....
....
Name of person to be contacted in case of injury ....
Address ....
....
....
Telephone number ....
Relationship to employee ....

FOR OFFICE USE ONLY

Date commenced work ....
Department ....
Works number ....

Documents checked ....
....

COLBAYNS HIGH SCHOOL
Clacton-on-Sea. CO15

Word Work

1

Copy these pairs of words into your book.

straight   strait   pique   peak
sore   soar   metal   mettle
vial   vile   medal   meddle
root   route   sight   site

Write sentences to show you understand the meaning of each word.

2

Choose the correct definition (meaning)
for each of the words printed below.
Write the word and its meaning in your book.

LACERATE
a cut badly
b decorate
c knit closely

AVID
a clumsy
b eager
c stupid

TRIVIAL
a unimportant
b expensive
c exhausting

PALTRY
a shave
b small, worthless
c educated

PRESS
a keep down
b improve
c take samples

SINISTER
a happy
b quiet
c evil

VERBOSE
a tame
b wordy
c simple

SERENITY
a calmness
b shrewdness
c thoughtfulness

DIVULGE
a make trouble
b make known
c enlarge

3

caddie
cobbler
confectioner
draper
stevedore
farrier
florist
grocer
joiner
hosier

Ten different kinds of job
are listed in the box.
Use a dictionary to find out
what is done by these workers.
Write the name of the job
and a description of it in your book.

PUZZLE PAGE

ANAGRAMS

Obtain a copy of this puzzle from your teacher.
(Headway English Copymasters 5, number 19.)

Look at the letters in the word **SAFER**.
If the order of the letters is changed the words **FARES**
and **FEARS** can be made.
The words **FARES** and **FEARS** are anagrams of the word
SAFER.

Complete the puzzle by writing two anagrams for each
of the words in the boxes.

M	E	A	T			T									
R	A	T	E			T									
N	E	S	T			S									
D	A	L	E			L									
M	A	L	E			M									
A	L	T	E	R		L									
S	A	T	I	N		S									
R	E	A	P	S		S									
B	A	R	E	D		B									
C	E	L	L	A	R		R								
G	A	N	D	E	R		G								

PROTEST in today's world

In Easter 1958 hundreds of people belonging to a newly-formed organisation went on a march in London. They marched from Trafalgar Square to the Atomic Weapons Research Establishment at Aldermaston in Berkshire. They were members of the Campaign for Nuclear Disarmament. C.N.D., as it has become known, is one of Britain's biggest protest movements. Its members want an end to the making of nuclear weapons and the preparation for a possible nuclear war.

Britain is a country which allows people to protest about things they think are wrong, on condition that the method of protest is within the law.

During this century there have been numerous protest movements in Britain. In 1903, Emmeline Pankhurst formed the Women's Social and Political Union (W.S.P.U.), whose members became known as the 'suffragettes'. The suffragettes were women who protested at the Government's refusal to allow them to vote in elections for Members of Parliament (MPs).

Sometimes a small protest movement grows into an international one. In this case protestors in several countries work together to bring about change. One of the best known international protest movements is called The Anti-Apartheid Movement. Apartheid is the name given to the separation of the white and black people of South Africa.

Most people believe it is every person's right to protest. However, people disagree sharply on the way a protest should be conducted. Protestors divide into two groups. There are those who believe in peaceful protest and those who believe it is necessary to break the law in order to bring about the changes they believe are right.

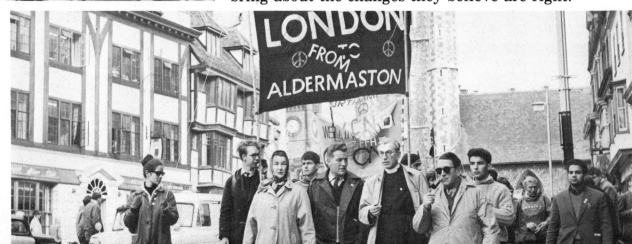

Read the section on PROTEST, then answer the questions.

1 What is CND?

2 What do CND members want banned?

3 CND members took part in a protest march in Easter 1958.
   a Where did the march begin?
   b Where did it end?
   c Why did they march to this particular Berkshire village?

4 Who was Emmeline Pankhurst?
   a What organisation did she form?
   b What were her supporters called?
   c About what did they protest?

5 Name one international protest movement.
   a What is its aim?
   b What is apartheid?

6 Under what condition are people allowed to protest
   freely in Britain?

7 Find in the passage a proper noun which is:
   a the name of a capital city
   b the name of a county
   c the name of a village
   d a Christian name
   e a surname.

8 CND stands for the Campaign for Nuclear Disarmament.
   What organisations are known by these abbreviations:
   TUC BBC EEC AA ITN RAC NATO

Word Work

1

| mason |
| milliner |
| optician |
| plumber |
| saddler |
| seamstress |
| steeplejack |
| stationer |
| tailor |
| locksmith |

Ten different kinds of job are listed in the box.
Use a dictionary to find out what is done by these workers.
Write the name of the job and a description of it in your book.

2

In each of these groups of words
there are two with similar meanings.
Copy the lists into your book.
Underline the similar words.

1 wages each pay withdrawal cheque
2 scarce frightened rare funny wicked
3 whip circus concert lash cry
4 angry tired careless irate probe
5 information admit detect confess persuade
6 enough thought sufficient tears plenty
7 conceal show bit cut hide stuff
8 scales folk show balance knife

3

Arrange the words printed below in two groups.
The first should contain words linked with the idea
of being joined, and the second group words linked with
the idea of being separate.
Use a dictionary if necessary.

independence	family	isolation	kinsfolk
allied	singular	unrelated	fraternal
solitary	tribe	insular	clan
group	individual	affiliated	detached

4

Copy these sentences into your book.
Choose the right word from those in the brackets to complete them.
a   David waited in a (cue queue) for a taxi.
b   Margaret designed a beautiful (freeze frieze) for her bedroom.
c   The tourist admired the (gilded guided) dome of the mosque.
d   Karl began a (libel liberal) action against the newspaper.
e   Cocaine is a (prescribed proscribed) drug which should only be taken
     under supervision.

5

Several words in English have more than one meaning.
Complete these pairs of sentences by putting in the same word.

a   The modern telephone has buttons to .... instead of a dial.
     The magazine was finally ready to go to ....

b   Colin was taken to .... for his part in the robbery.
     There was a full size tennis .... at the hotel.

c   The body of the Queen will .... in state for the next five days.
     David told a .... to avoid punishment.

d   The plane came in to .... at Manchester airport.
     The farmer bought some .... at the auction.

6

Here are five words associated with speech:

asked   repeated   demanded   whispered   shouted

Which of the words would you use to show:

a   the speaker was speaking very loudly
b   the speaker was talking very quietly
c   the speaker wanted information
d   the speaker was making a forceful request
e   the speaker was giving out information again

Kinds of Poetry — The Epitaph

An epitaph is a short speech or passage written
to keep alive the memory of a dead person.
They are often engraved on tombstones.
Surprisingly, some epitaphs are unkind and insulting.
Here are some humorous examples:

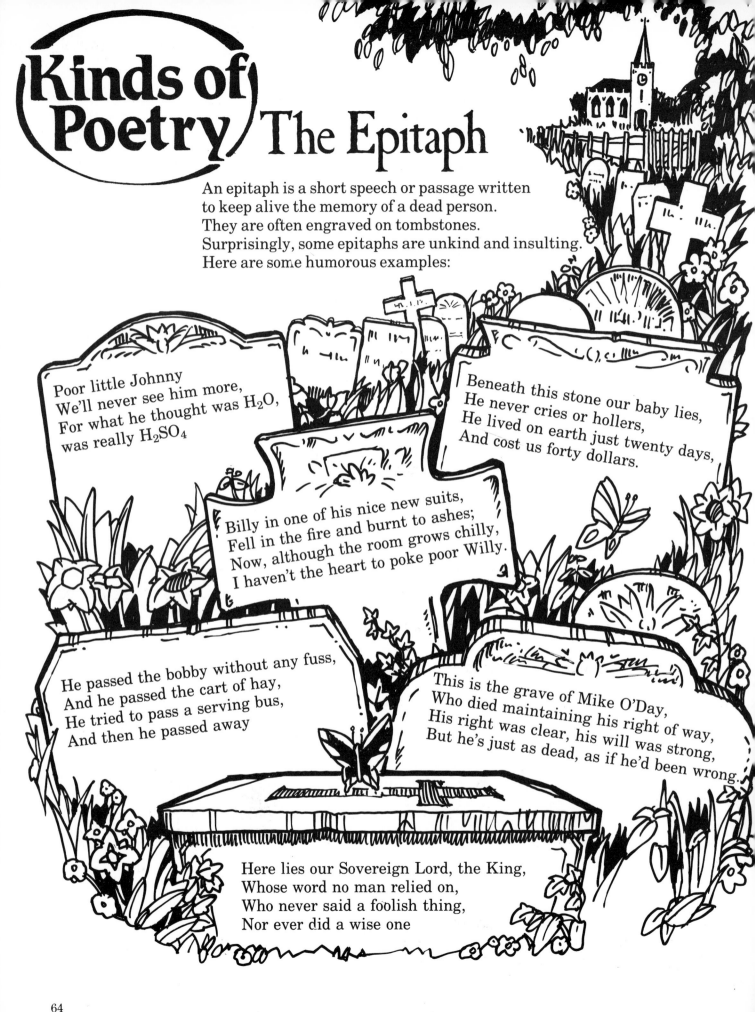

Poor little Johnny
We'll never see him more,
For what he thought was H_2O,
was really H_2SO_4

Beneath this stone our baby lies,
He never cries or hollers,
He lived on earth just twenty days,
And cost us forty dollars.

Billy in one of his nice new suits,
Fell in the fire and burnt to ashes;
Now, although the room grows chilly,
I haven't the heart to poke poor Willy.

He passed the bobby without any fuss,
And he passed the cart of hay,
He tried to pass a serving bus,
And then he passed away

This is the grave of Mike O'Day,
Who died maintaining his right of way,
His right was clear, his will was strong,
But he's just as dead, as if he'd been wrong.

Here lies our Sovereign Lord, the King,
Whose word no man relied on,
Who never said a foolish thing,
Nor ever did a wise one

Read the epitaphs then answer the questions.

1　Explain the symbols H_2O and H_2SO_4.

2　What was the caused of Johnny's death?

3　Bobby is the nickname for a policeman.
　Make a list of other nicknames used for police
　persons.

4　What does a baby do when it 'hollers'?

5　What word suggests that the epitaph about the baby
　was written by an American?

6　In the epitaph about the king, find a word
　which is the opposite of foolish.

7　In the epitaph about Mike O'Day, find words which
　mean:

　keeping up　burial place　not alive

8　In the epitaph about the boy falling in the fire,
　Billy and Willy are abbreviations for the name
　William.

　Write these names in full: Di, Phil, Nick, Penny,
　Sue, Chris, Mike

Write the story of how you think Mike O'Day lost
his life.
What lesson is to be learnt from the story?

Copy into your notebook the three epitaphs
you find most amusing.
Look in a poetry book for other epitaphs.

Draw a picture of a tombstone.
Write on it an epitaph for an imaginary person.
It is possible to make up an epitaph about people
who do particular jobs: doctors, teachers, postmen,
etc.

Writing Work

PRODUCING A CLASS MAGAZINE

Producing a class magazine is a good way of showing how
well you can write.
A magazine is also a good way of telling others
about your interests, hobbies and activities.
First it is necessary to choose an Editor and an assistant.
They will be the people responsible for selecting what will be
included in the magazine and in what order
the items should appear.
Here are some ideas for a class magazine:

STORIES
These must not be too long. They can be about fictitious
events, real events, for example stories about animals,
holidays.

FEATURE ARTICLES
These should be about hobbies, cookery, crafts, pop
groups, fashion, plays.

SPORT
These articles should be about facilities for sport either at school
or in your area. The sport section might include a report
on an important match which has been played.

POETRY
A poem specially written for the magazine
would be a welcome contribution.

LETTERS
Write a letter to the Editor about the things that interest you.
State your views about local and national events, or people.
These letters should be printed
on a 'Letters to the Editor' page.

ADVERTISEMENTS
Find out if anyone has anything for sale
or a service they are willing to give.

HUMOUR
These are very short stories, jokes and witty sayings.

Choose one of the above headings.
Write a contribution for your class magazine.

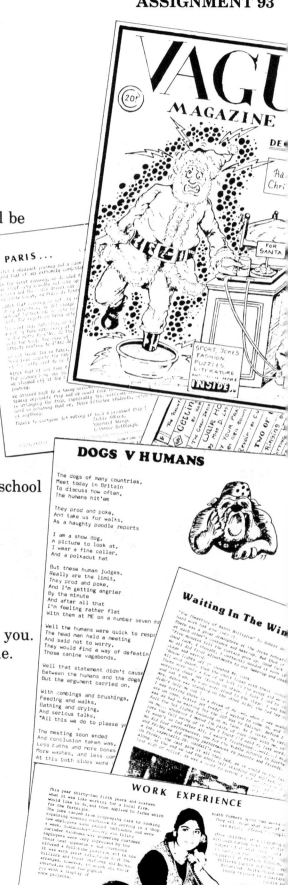

66

PUZZLE PAGE

Obtain a copy of this puzzle from your teacher. (Headway
English copymasters 5, number 20.
Extra puzzles numbers 21 and 22.)
Complete the crossword.

CLUES ACROSS

1 To persuade
4 Book of maps
6 A donkey
9 To escape
10 Ready to be picked
11 to brown the skin
13 Payment
15 Pleasant
16 Pleasurable activity
19 A small breed of horse
22 Wandering people
23 Egypt's capital
25 Someone who will
provide a testimonial
26 A container for liquids

CLUES DOWN

1 Pure
2 To give permission
3 Disturbing experience
5 To wander across country
7 A bursting one is a sign
of the coming of Spring
8 Short poem
12 Hard, uncaring
14 A taxi is sometimes called
this.
17 Worried
18 Part of the arm
20 A work of fiction
21 To skip, frolic
24 Wet flat land

Ideas in bronze and stone —Henry Moore, sculptor—

Sculpture can depict a wide variety of ideas, people or things. It might commemorate a famous person, such as the statue of Winston Churchill, the British wartime leader; or a memorable event, for example the Dutch sculpture illustrated below. The artist is expressing his idea of the horror of war through the image of terrified people trying to protect themselves from falling bombs.

Sculptors may work in two different ways. Sometimes they build up their work by joining together and shaping pieces of the material they are using. At other times, they take a large piece of material and chisel it down to the size and shape they require. The first way of working is called modelling, the second method is called carving.

The work of sculptor Henry Moore is found in many parts of the world. He was born in Castleford in 1898 and died in 1986. Moore particularly liked using bronze because this metal is largely unaffected by the weather. It is therefore an ideal material for standing in the parks and other open spaces which he favoured for displaying his work.

He liked people to think his shapes had come about by the work of the wind and rain, rather than having been created by an artist. Large holes and caverns are a feature of his work. He used to say that these reminded him of the caves in the Yorkshire hills where he lived and played as a child.

Sculpture in Rotterdam, Holland.

Henry Moore's sculpture, King and Queen, in Dumfries, Scotland.

Read about the work of the sculptor, then answer these questions.

ASSIGNMENT 95

1 Who is the famous British sculptor named in the passage?

2 What metal did this sculptor often select for his work?
   Why was it chosen?

3 In what kind of situation did this sculptor like to see his work?

4 Large holes are sometimes a feature of Henry Moore's work.
   What explanation is given for this?

5 What is meant by
   a modelling a sculpture
   b carving a sculpture?

6 In the passage give an example of a noun which is:
   a the name of a tool
   b the name of a metal
   c the name of a town
   d the name of an occupation

7 Give an example of a piece of scultpure
   made to remind us of a famous person.

8 Which piece of sculpture expresses an artist's idea.

9 A sculptor uses a chisel in his work.
   Who would use the following:
   hoe   spanner   typewriter   scalpel
   computer   calculator   stethoscope

LIFE SKILLS

YOUR PERSONAL PROFILE

Your personal profile is a word picture of yourself.

Before making a decision about what you will do
when you leave school it is a good idea
to have a clear understanding of your personality,
i.e. the kind of person you are.

You will need to know your strengths and weaknesses
– your ability to read, write, to speak correctly, to
work with figures and handle money.

Obtain a copy from your teacher
of the PERSONAL PROFILE RECORD SHEETS.
(Headway English Copymasters 5, numbers 23 and 24.)
Complete the profile.
Give yourself a mark out of ten for how well you think
you complete each task.

PART 1

PROFILE RECORD CARD

SURNAME ....

FIRST NAME(S) ....

DATE OF BIRTH ....

ADDRESS ....

....

....

TELEPHONE NUMBER ....

NAME OF SCHOOL ....

SCHOOL ADDRESS ....

....

....

NAME OF SCHOOL COUNSELLOR/CAREERS TEACHER.

....

DISABILITY AND WEAKNESSES ....

....

....

LIFE SKILLS

PART 2

COMMUNICATION WITH OTHERS

Is your handwriting clear and accurate?	
Is your spelling accurate?	
Can you write a sentence in answer to a question?	
Would you find it easy to write a description of an event?	
Can you use a telephone?	
Could you look up a telephone number without difficulty?	
Can you give clear directions?	
Do you find it easy to take a message?	
Can you write a formal letter?	
Can you read a newspaper?	
Do you find it easy to fill in forms?	

PART 3

NUMBER SKILLS

Can you add and subtract single numbers in your head?	
Can you add and subtract double numbers in your head?	
Can you do simple written addition, subtraction, multiplication and division?	
Do you know your 'tables'?	
Can you work our change from a pound (£)	
Can you work out change from £5?	
Can you read a bus or train time-table?	
Can you measure in yards, feet and inches?	
Can you measure in millimetres, centimetres and metres?	
Can you weigh in pounds and ounces?	
Can you weigh in grams and kilograms?	
Can you do simple fractions?	

LIFE SKILLS

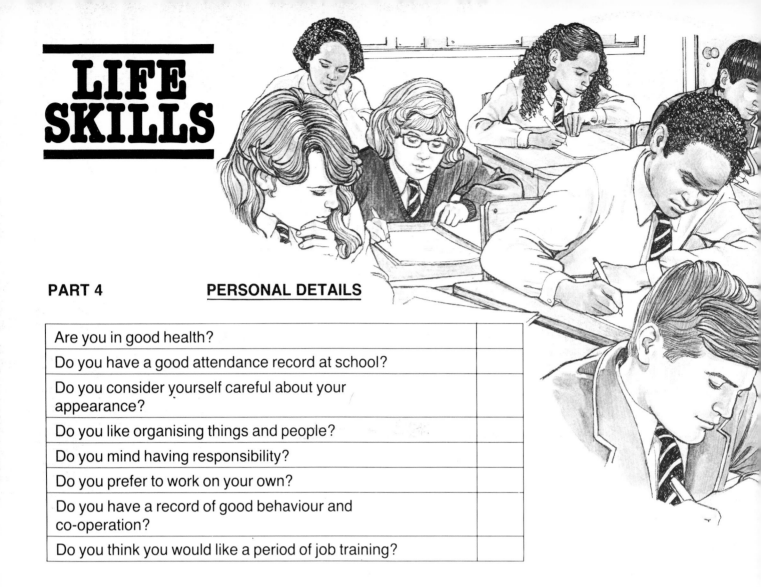

PART 4   <u>PERSONAL DETAILS</u>

Are you in good health?	
Do you have a good attendance record at school?	
Do you consider yourself careful about your appearance?	
Do you like organising things and people?	
Do you mind having responsibility?	
Do you prefer to work on your own?	
Do you have a record of good behaviour and co-operation?	
Do you think you would like a period of job training?	

ASSIGNMENT 97

DISCUSSION
When you have completed your profile,
discuss it with your teacher.
How far does your teacher's assessment agree with yours?
Discuss what you feel about leaving school
with your teacher and the rest of your group.
Suggest points in favour of leaving,
of staying on or going to a college or YTS scheme.

ASSIGNMENT 98

Write about leaving school.
Write about what you hope to do in the future.

Look back over your years at school.
Write your autobiography to date.
Record not only events but also impressions.
Write about both good and bad memories.

Kinds of Poetry

HAIKU

Haiku poems are always short. They were first composed by the Japanese and consist of only seventeen syllables. The syllables of a haiku are usually arranged into three lines, with five syllables on the first line, seven syllables on the second line, and five syllables on the third line. There is no rhyme.

A haiku can be used to record a fleeting moment or a vivid image. Here are some examples of haiku poems.

The Birds
The sun is cool now,
In a sky of fluffy clouds,
Where the birds flutter.

The Robin
Regard his bright breast,
Listen to his lovely song,
Oh, No! Now he's gone.

The Fox
Brown as a hazel nut
Furry as a squirrel's tail,
Dashing through the woods.

The Snail
Down a garden path,
A very slow snail doth stroll
Pleased to be alive.

Copy these poems into your poetry book.
Illustrate each one with a coloured drawing.

ASSIGNMENT 99

Look in poetry books for other haiku poems.
Copy those you like into your book.

ASSIGNMENT 100

Try writing your own haiku.
Here are some suggested topics.

a baby's smile	a baby's first step	the first crocus
falling asleep	a cow and calf	shire horses
a hedgehog	catkins	old people talking

Word Work

1

MORE ABBREVIATIONS

The name of the county is often abbreviated in a written address.
The position of twenty counties of England and Wales have been marked on this map.
Counties and regions of Northern Ireland and Scotland are rarely abbreviated.
Use an atlas to find the names of these counties. Then match each county name with its abbreviated form

GLOS
WILTS
HANTS
M. GLAM
BERKS
HERTS
OXON
LANCS
DERBYS
LINCS
BUCKS
CAMBS
HERF & WORCS
LEICS
W. MID
NORTHUMB
NORTHANTS
NOTTS
N. YORKS
WARWICKS

2

The abbreviation and the title of these organisations have been mixed up.
Match each title with its correct abbreviation.

Manpower Services Commission	NSPCC
Youth Training Scheme	GCSE
Department of Health & Social Security	MSC
North Atlantic Treaty Organisation	NATO
General Certificate of Secondary Education	YTS
European Economic Community (Common Market)	EEC
National Society for the Prevention of Cruelty to Children.	DHSS

PUZZLE PAGE

Ask your teacher for a copy of this puzzle.
(Headway English Copymasters 5, number 25).
Fit the words into the puzzle.
Fit the words clockwise, so that the last two letters of
one word, become the first two letters of the next.

almost	sealed	icicle	usage	nasturium
decimetre	terminal	lyric	cenotaph	revolve
estimate	umbrella	photostat	erode	strength
hyena	atrocious	shapely	greenhouse	ulcer
leaves	education	thankful	languish	vengeance
only	geography			

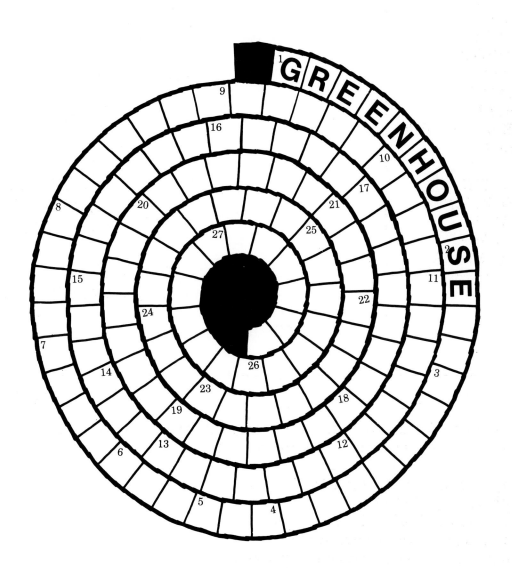

Is it Mammal or Reptile?
THE AUSTRALIAN PLATYPUS

About 2,000 million years ago there lived a group of animals which were half-reptile and half-mammal. Only a few of these, nature's oddities, survive. One of them is the Australian platypus.

Like most mammals, the body of the platypus is covered with hair. The short velvet-like hair is brown on the back and turns to grey on the undertside. The animal is often called the 'duckbill' because it has a large snout which looks like a duck's beak.

The female feeds her young with her own milk but, unlike other mammals, she does not give birth to young ones. Instead she builds a nest into which she lays her eggs. During September, the female can be observed digging out a nest burrow, into which she will lay up to three soft-shelled white eggs. After hatching, the female protects the young in the nest for about three months before they are allowed to wander away.

The male platypus is about two feet in length, the female is slightly shorter. Both have round heads and no visible ears. The webbed feet have five sharp claws. The animal is able to fold away this webbing when it wants to dig or claw.

The platypus is found beside rivers and lakes in most parts of Australia. They remain in their burrows by day, coming out in the evening to feed on worms, insects and fresh crayfish. They are strong swimmers, swinging their head from side to side as they move through the water.

Read about the platypus, then answer the following questions.

1 Why is the platypus an unusual animal?

2 Use your dictionary to find out the meaning of:
   mammal, reptile.

3 In which country is the platypus found?

4 Describe the animal.

5 Why is the animal often called a Duckbill?

6 In what way does the animal resemble a mammal?

7 In what way does the platypus differ from a mammal?

8 On what does the animal feed?

9 Habitat means where a plant or animal lives.
   Describe the habitat of the platypus.

10 Find words and phrases in the passage which mean:
    a unusual   b suckle
    c seen   d to stay inside

Draw a picture of an Australian platypus.

Word Work

1

The following sentences do not mean exactly what they say.
Explain the phrases in italics in each sentence:

1 My mother kept *a stiff upper lip*.
2 My friend's *heart was in her shoes*.
3 David is *too big for his boots*.
4 Khaled has *turned over a new leaf*.
5 The arrested man *slipped through the fingers* of the detective.
6 My father decided it was time *to save for a rainy day*.

2

Copy these sentences into your book.
Choose the right word from those in the brackets.
Use a dictionary, if necessary, to find the meaning of the words.

1 Aluminium is a (malleable   malignant) metal.
2 The (council   counsel) offices are in the High Street.
3 Jane was in (imminent   eminent) danger of drowning.
4 A (statute   statue) of the general was erected in the Square.
5 I shall go to America for my (vacation   vocation).
6 Karen plays the (cymbals   symbols) in the orchestra.

3

Five of the words in the list below have the same meaning
as HUMOROUS.
Find the words. Use your dictionary if necessary.

farcical   rowdy
tedious   droll
laughable   humdrum
despicable   sluggish
witty   jocular

Write five sentences.
Use one of the words in each sentence.

78

4

Use another verb instead of **GOT** and **GET**
in the following sentences:

1   I shall get there at three o'clock.
2   The prisoner got clean away.
3   Get me an evening paper.
4   The cowboy got the steer with his rope.
5   We got the criminal after a long search.
6   I do not get what you mean.
7   Will you get out of my way, please.
8   Can I get some writing paper from the shop?

5

The word underlined in each of the sentences
is incorrect.
The correct word is one which looks similar.
Copy and correct the sentences.

a   My father has bought a new *suit* for the lounge.
b   Halil was at a *loss* end so he went into the
    museum.
c   Kirstey and Nigel have *adopted* a baby.
d   Rao came *formerly* dressed to the party.
e   Janet put on her best *cloths* for the interview.
f   The legs of the chair were carved on the *lath*.
g   Leico has become a *perfect* at Woolaston School.

6

Copy these sentences into your book.
Underline the word in each sentence which is not
needed.

a   A huge multitude thronged the cathedral square.
b   The young baby cried all night.
c   The winding road has many bends.
d   I myself baked Rajiv's birthday cake.
e   In what kind of situation did Moore like to see his
    work situated.

Word Work

7

Arrange these words into two groups. The first should
contain words which suggest AGREEMENT.
The second group words which suggest DISAGREEMENT.

unity	conflict	hostility	conformity	matching
solidarity	union	consistent	disharmony	row
quarrel	bickering	dissenting	unanimous	wrangling

Choose three 'agreement' words and three 'disagreement' words,
then write sentences. Use one word in each sentence.

8

Add a prefix to each of the words below
in order to make a word of opposite meaning.

possible	behave	please	perfect
reasonable	responsible	observed	trust

Write eight sentences.
Use one of the words you have made in each sentence.

9

Copy these sentences into your book.
Choose the correct word from those in the brackets
to complete the sentences.

1 Rixi was (borne   born) across the river on a raft.
2 Sanji bought a (pear   pair) of shoes in the market.
3 All letters coming out of the prison were (censored   censured).
4 Ian wore a snorkel suit while diving to see the beautiful
   (corral   coral) formations.
5 Nigel became angry and began to wave his
   (clenched   clinched) fist.

Choose the correct meaning for each of these words.

RAMPANT
a stubborn
b curious
c unchecked

EMIT
a irritate
b send out
c make easy

SCUTTLE
a sleep soundly
b to sink on purpose
c to pray

FISSURE
a flashy dress
b a deep crack
c a painful sore

CASSOCK
a priest's gown
b a singing bird
c a kind of thermometer

INDOLENT
a hopeless
b lazy
c cruel

MAIM
a to beautify
b to attack
c to cripple

FOIBLE
a weakness
b poison
c decoration

PENSIVE
a to be thoughtful
b to be angry
c to be untidy

Choose any six of the above words.
Write sentences using one of the words chosen in each sentence.

Match each word with its meaning.

FLUFFY   to persuade
REPAY   to squeeze together
CONVINCE   to suffocate
COMPRESS   soft and light
ACCOMPLISH   to be gloomy
ASPHYXIATE   give back
CONFUSED   dangerous
PESSIMISTIC   to pay no attention
HAZARDOUS   to be mixed up
DISREGARD   to finish

Writing Work

SENDING A POSTCARD

Postcards are used to send short messages
which are not of a private or confidential nature.
There are two kinds of postcard, the 'picture postcard'
and the 'plain postcard'.
Picture postcards are mostly sent by people on holiday.
They usually consist of a coloured photograph
of the holiday resort.
Another sort of picture postcard is the cartoon type.
This kind of card has a coloured cartoon picture
and a caption on the front.
Traditionally, both the subject of the picture
and the message are often quite rude.
Here are two examples of picture postcards
traditionally favoured by holiday-makers.

Write postcard messages for the following:
1   to your parents, telling them of your arrival
    at your holiday resort
2   to a member of the tennis club committee
    giving notice of a meeting
3   to the Gas Board, requesting a fitter to call
    at your house to service a gas fire
4   to your dentist cancelling an appointment.

The plain postcard is often used for short messages:
Plain postcards are used:
a   to confirm appointments
b   to give notice of meetings
c   as a reminder
d   to arrange sports fixtures
c   to give small pieces of information.

Here are two examples of postcard messages.

When writing a postcard it is not necessary to begin
with an opening like Dear Sir or Dear Dad.
Neither is it necessary to put your address, or the name
and address of the person to whom you are writing,
at the top of the card.

MATHS VOCABULARY

Ask your teacher for a copy of this puzzle. (Headway English Copymasters 5, number 26. Extra puzzle numbers 27, 28 and 29). Can you find the twenty five MATHS WORDS hidden in the puzzle. As you find each one, write the word in your book.

P	G	R	T	R	I	F	P	E	R	I	M
O	A	D	D	I	T	I	O	N	L	G	E
U	S	F	A	D	S	G	U	P	I	N	T
N	U	S	R	Y	A	U	A	F	T	A	E
D	B	U	F	A	B	R	C	R	R	N	R
G	T	B	I	R	C	E	E	A	E	G	G
R	R	T	G	D	P	T	E	A	F	L	A
A	A	O	U	S	I	D	I	A	R	E	L
P	C	M	I	L	E	S	G	O	H	I	L
H	T	G	R	D	O	L	I	T	N	N	O
M	U	L	T	I	P	L	Y	F	R	C	N
D	C	D	E	V	F	E	E	L	E	H	B
E	O	C	C	I	R	C	L	E	T	E	O
C	S	G	A	D	L	L	O	S	N	S	T
S	H	A	P	E	S	L	A	S	T	W	A
C	D	E	C	I	A	M	U	A	M	E	N
T	E	Y	A	V	L	I	R	D	E	I	G
R	S	N	O	A	D	G	R	A	T	G	E
I	P	H	T	A	A	D	S	G	R	H	N
A	A	O	R	I	M	E	T	R	E	T	T
N	T	M	E	T	C	E	N	A	T	I	M
G	L	E	T	R	A	P	I	M	Z	I	M

Addition
Angle
Area
Circle
Divide
Figure
Fraction
Gallon
Gram
Graph
Inches
Litre
Metre
Mile
Multiply
Oval
Pint
Pound
Radius
Shapes
Subtract
Tangent
Total
Weight
Yard

Machu Picchu... The lost city of the Incas

Today, the Inca people are mostly poor and uneducated. They live in mud-hut villages among the Andes, the high mountain range of South America. Until about four hundred years ago they were a proud people, the rulers of a great, fabulously rich empire. At the height of their power, they lived in splendid cities. They were skilful engineers, who built aqueducts to carry water, and roads which made communication possible throughout the empire. Their mines produced huge quantities of gold and silver. It was this seemingly endless wealth which made them a prey to invaders in the sixteenth century.

Within the space of just fifty years the kingdom of the Incas was destroyed by invading Spaniards. Their cities were ruined, their leaders killed and their great wealth taken from them and shipped to Spain. The Incas became a poor, almost forgotten people.

A century ago, rumour began to spread that deep inside the jungles, lying on the lower slopes of the Andes, there still existed an Inca city called Machu Picchu, with its great wealth intact. Several explorers set off to find the lost city and some died in the search, but eventually one man was successful. His name was Hiram Bingham.

Bingham discovered Machu Picchu built on a narrow ledge, in the mountains of the country we call Peru. Bingham found the great palace of the Inca king, the magnificent temple of the sun god, and terraces of once beautiful homes surrounded by strong defences. It seemed that everything was there except what Bingham wanted most – the gold and silver treasure.

Read about Machu Picchu, the lost city of the Incas, then answer these questions.

1 What and where are the Andes? In what country are they found?
2 Who are the Incas?
3 Describe the present state of these people.
4 Were they always like this?
5 What made them a prey to invaders?
6 Who defeated the Inca people and raided their treasure?
7 What is the name of the 'lost city of the Incas'?
8 What did rumour say about this city?
9 Did the rumour prove to be true?
10 Who discovered Machu Picchu?
11 In which country are the ruins found?
12 Why is Spanish spoken in Peru today?
13 Which words in the passage mean something similar to:

   a gossip   d at last
   b found   e enclosed
   c victim   f undisturbed

14 An adjective describes a noun. Find adjectives in the passage which describe these nouns:

cities	palace	defences	palace
temple	Andes	people	defences

Machu Picchu, Peru.

1 Write in your book the names of the days of the week.

2 Copy these sentences into your book.
Underline the nouns in each sentence.
a Nadia had a chicken for her dinner.
b Rangi has a white turban.
c David sailed from Southampton in the beautiful liner.
d Margaret is wearing a red dress,
black stockings and red shoes.

3 Use 'a' or 'an' to complete these sentences.
a ...... elephant is ...... big animal.
b I carry ...... umbrella when ...... storm looks
threatening.
c There was ...... empty seat on top of the bus.

4 Write out the names of the numbers from one to ten.

5 Complete these sentences.
a The opposite of east is ....

b The opposite of north is ....

c The opposite of tame is ....

d The opposite of sharp is ....

e The opposite of straight is ....

f The opposite of slack is ....

6 Write in your book the names
of the first six months of the year.

7 Choose the right word.
a I often (play   plan   plant) in the park.
b Caroline has drawn a (plan   plank   plastic)
of the classroom.
c The two friends had a (queen   quarrel   quick)
during the party
d St. Peter's School came top in the 'Brain of Britain'
(quarrel   quiz   queue).

8   Write the names of the last six months of the year
    in your book.

9   Write the plural of each of these words:
    flower   brush   fox   knife   baby
    army   roof   fly   valley   load

10 Write the singular of each of these words:
    roses   ladies   loaves knives
    wives   women   boats   fishermen

11 Arrange these words in alphabetical order:
    poem   ripe   snow   nobody
    cabin   abandon   dish   which
    baby   emerald   goal   justice
    zebra   violet   ivory   under
    kilt   orange   man   happy
    length   year   flesh   queen
    nurse   tomato   x-ray

12 Write a letter congratulating a friend
    on passing the GCSE.
    or
    Write a letter congratulating a friend on
    becoming engaged.

13 Match each of these words with its meaning.
    clock   hide   midnight   secret   urgent

    a   Something you do not want others to know about
    b   Used to tell the time
    c   To put out of sight
    d   Needing to be done at once
    e   Twelve o'clock at night.

14 Copy these sentences into your book.
    Underline the adjectives in each sentence.

    a   The red flag flew over the old castle.
    b   The young girl came to the market to sell
        her fresh vegetables.
    c   A smart young man wearing blue trousers
        carried my heavy cases into the large hotel.

15 Copy and correct these sentences.
   a dr auzair lives at 26 gordon road newtown
   b mrs d e anderson is the school secretary
   c mr and mrs colin brown are staying at the hotel
   d the rev dr owen is the minister at st pauls church

16 Rewrite these sentences.
   Use one of the words taken from the list to replace
   the words underlined.
   collided delighted misfortune adults
   a Anne was *very pleased* with her present.
   b The two cars *banged together* on the road.
   c All the *grown ups* were served first at the party.
   d Sangi had the *bad luck* to be ill during the match.

17 Choose the best definition for each word printed
   in CAPITAL LETTERS.

   COSY   **BASHFUL**   **FROWN**
   a comfortable   a harmful   a to be busy
   b cold   b shy   b to be angry
   c itching   c poor   c to look displeased

18 Write out the following:
   a Your full name
   b Your address
   c Your date of birth (in words)
   d The name of your school
   e The address of your school
   f The name and address of your doctor.

19 Make a list of eight colours.

20 Write about a book you have recently read.
   a Give the title
   b Make a list of the main characters
   c State briefly what the story is about

21 Each of these pairs of words sound the same
    but their meanings are very different.
    Write sentences to show you understand the meaning
    of each word.
    key ....quay   knight ....night
    plain ....plane   buoy ....boy
    reigns ....reins   horse ....hoarse
    metal ....mettle   fair ....fare

22 Copy these sentences into your book.
    Change the verb in each sentence into the PAST
    TENSE.
    a I am going to the disco.
    b We shall all go to church on Sunday.
    c The plane from Paris will arrive at 4 o'clock.

23 Copy these sentences into your book.
    Change the verb in each sentence
    into the FUTURE tense.
    a I left school at Easter.
    b We all walked along the river bank.
    c They came early for dinner.

24 Read this advertisement.

> **PINK WALLFLOWERS**
>
> Very hardy and rare, grown from selected
> seed. Plant outdoors now for early display
> of large flowers.
> **Will flower for six months.**
>
> **Plants 25 for £2.50, 50 for £4.50.**
> Carriage paid.
> Hundreds of testimonials.
> T. C. Grey, F R H S. Grange Nursery,
> Wisbech, Cambs.

    Write a letter in answer to this advertisement.
    Order 50 plants.

25 A year later you see the same advertisement.
    Write a letter of complaint, saying that the plants
    you received were not hardy, were yellow and bloomed
    for only three weeks.

This extract is part of a poem by Charles Causley.
Read the poem then answer the questions.

Timothy Winters comes to school
With eyes as wide as a football pool,
Ears like bombs and teeth like splinters;
A blitz of a boy is Timothy Winters.

His belly is white, his neck is dark,
And his hair is an exclamation mark.
His clothes are enough to scare a crow,
And through his trousers, the wild wind blows.

When teacher talks, he won't hear a word,
And he shoots down dead the arithmetic bird,
He licks the patterns off his plate
And he's not even heard of the Welfare state.

Timothy Winters has bloody feet,
And he lives in a house on Suez street,
He sleeps in a sack on the kitchen floor
And they say there aren't boys like him any more.

Old man Winters likes his beer,
And his missus ran off with a bombardier,
Grandma sits in the grate with a gin,
And Timothy's dosed with an aspirin.

1   It is suggested that modern poets like to write
    about squalor rather than pleasant situations.
    Is this true of this poem?
    Write out two lines which suggest Timothy comes
    from a poor home.

2   Which lines suggest Timothy is not interested
    in school?

3   Explain the lines:
    'He's not even heard of the Welfare state'
    'His missus ran off with a bombardier'

4   What details in the poem make you feel sorry
    for Timothy?

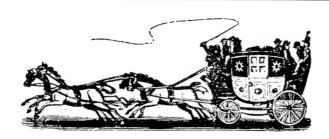

1   The following ten proverbs (sayings) can be divided
    into five pairs, each pair having a similar meaning.

    Pair-off the sayings.

    Write them in your book.
    a Look before you leap.
    b It's an ill wind that blows nobody any good.
    c Opportunity only knocks once.
    d Faint heart never won a fair lady.
    e Nothing ventured, nothing gained.
    f Every cloud has a silver lining.
    g A pot shouldn't call a kettle black.
    h Fools rush in where angels fear to tread.
    i Make hay while the sun shines.
    j People who live in glasshouses shouldn't throw
       stones.

2   In a few sentences, describe the meaning of any two
    of the above proverbs.

3   From the verbs (action words) printed on the right,
    select the verb nearest in meaning to the one printed
    in CAPITAL LETTERS.

    QUARREL ....argue   converse   discuss   speak.
    SURROUND ....beseige   attack   encircle   surrender.
    POSTPONE ....delay   cancel   adjourn   finish.
    ASKED ....repeated   requested   mumbled   muttered.
    CANTERED ....galloped   stampeded   ambled   trotted.

4   In each of the following lists two words are similar
    in meaning.
    Copy the lists into your book.
    Underline the words which are similar in meaning.
    a draw   join   bring   help   stay   connect.
    b lost   mistaken   spoiled   hidden   spent   concealed
    c determine   reside   declare   resolve   depend   succeed
    d clogs   dress   feet   sandals   cardigan   socks
    e balance   scales   weight   heavy   light
    f fiction   page   novel   letter   ink   pen

5   Copy these sentences into your book.
    Underline the PRONOUN in each one.
    a   Diana did her homework before she went to the baths.
    b   Stephen and Paul repaired their bikes in the garden.
    c   We must hurry or you will miss the bus.

6   Complete these sentences by using a suitable
    CONJUNCTION.
    a   It is cold today .... it is raining.
    b   Alison felt ill .... she continued around the track.
    c   Nigel was late for school .... the bus broke down.

7   Read this short poem.

    There was a young pig from Brynamon,
        Who carried a nice piece of gammon,
        With cutlets and chops,
        For pork butchers' shops   *A. M. Prosser*
    And a few shapely bones with some ham on.

    a   What is gammon?
    b   What occupation is mentioned in the poem?
    c   What name is given to this short, funny kind of
        poem?

8   Write a letter to a friend in hospital – regret that
    your friend is ill – inquire if an operation will be
    necessary – ask about visiting hours – pass on a bit
    of news which you think might interest your friend.

9   Write a diary for the last three days.
    Write about four sentences for each day.
    Write about school, games played, leisure activities,
    programmes seen on TV.

10 Copy these sentences into your notebook.
    Change the words underlined in each sentence for
    one of the words below:
    coarse   casual   censured   cowered   site
    contrasted   confidant   canvassing

a   Floyd came to the reception dressed in *informal
    colourful, comfortable* clothes.

b   Alex knocked on every door in Redcar Street,
    asking for support for the Greenleaf candidate.

c   Sean *pointed out the differences between*
    the two types of washing machine.

d   Angela and Greg drove to the *plot on the building
    development* where their house was being erected.

e   Winston *crouched down, covering his head*
    as the debris fell about him.

f   Jamie became Mary's *trusted friend and adviser*
    after she had her divorce.

g   Heather was described by her workmates
    as a *vulgar, rough, loud mouthed* sort of girl.

h   Ian was *reported and disciplined* for leaving
    the cab of his lorry unlocked.

11 Choose the best word taken from those in the brackets
    to complete the following comparisons.
    a   as flat as a .... (board   saucer
        pancake   sheet)
    b   as steady as a .... (cliff   rock   boulder   stone)
    c   as smooth as .... (velvet   grass   glass   cotton)
    d   as sweet as .... (jam   sugar   honey   mutton)
    e   as swift as a .... (horse   hound   deer   sprinter)
    f   as cunning as a .... (fox   lion   tiger   cat)

12 Many words in English have more than one
meaning e.g.
We all stood in a *ring*.
I told David to *ring* the bell.

Complete each pair of sentences by supplying
the same word.

a Roger's .... is coming up at the Old Bailey
in July.
Arjun carried Sarah's .... into the house.

b The gold .... was left on the table.
The policeman kept .... on the flat.

c We turned .... at the end of the road.
Ibraham has .... the building.

d There were no seats free so we had to ....
A small wooden .... stood in the corner of the hall.

e Mrs Thatcher was the first woman in Britain
to hold the .... of Prime Minister.
Mary is the school secretary, her .... is along the
corridor.

---

13 Write these words in your book in the form of a list.

caught drowned reign breath goal
flower pass crest spelling station

At the side of each word write
two others which rhyme with it.

---

14 Write a formal letter in reply
to this advertisement.

> **Young person wanted** for general warehouse
> work. Some stock control, filing
> and record keeping. **Apply: Personnel
> Officer, Kempton Motor Parts, Kirby Road,
> Preston. Lancs. LA2. 9PG.**

Address an envelope for your application.

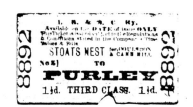

15   Write in full the following abbreviations:
     NUR NUPE NUM AUEW TGWU
     They are all the initials of British Trade Unions.

16   Janet Evans lives at Cherry Tree Estate.
     Her nearest bus stop is the Red Lion.
     She is going to work for Kempton Motor Parts.
     The warehouse is just three minutes away
     from the Greenmeadow stop.
     Her house is five minutes away from the Red Lion.
     Janet has to clock in by 7.30 a.m.

ROUTE 242			
Lodge Hall Garage	06.35	06.50	07.05
Royal Lane	06.40	06.55	07.10
Red Lion	06.43	06.58	07.13
Blackpond Rd	06.47	07.02	07.17
Market Sq.	06.54	07.09	07.24
Kingtown Station	06.59	07.14	07.29
Greenmeadow Lane	07.05	07.20	07.35
Park Street	07.10	07.25	07.40

Read the time-table, then answer the following
questions.

1   Which bus will get Janet to work on time?
2   About what time will she need to leave home?
3   Which stop is the most suitable for Kempton
    Motor Parts?
4   How long does the journey take?
5   How much time has Janet to get from the bus
    stop to her place of work?
6   If she missed the bus, how long would she have
    to wait for the next?

PUZZLE PAGE

GIANT CROSSWORD
Ask your teacher for a copy of this puzzle.
(Headway English Copymasters 5, number 30).
Complete the crossword

CLUES ACROSS

1   Poem with an old story.
5   Variety of stone with
    very smooth surface.
6   British sculptor.
8   Opposite of day.
10 Dangerous substance.
12 Parents come to meetings
    of this association.
13 Short poem, in Japanese style.
14 Variety of fish.
17 Contained in an atlas.
19 Royal title of the kings of Egypt.
20 Not far.
22 Small hotel.
23 Famous rat catcher.

CLUES DOWN

1   Variety of shark.
2   Short kind of poem.
3   To pull along the ground.
4   Australian creature – a half reptile.
5   Read in a restaurant.
7   Variety of wood used in carving.
9   Cunning animal.
11 Welsh delicacy.
14 German city – once rat infested.
15 What is left after something is burnt.
16 To persuade.
18 Mars is one.
19 Small variety of horse.
21 fifth form exam. Abbreviation.

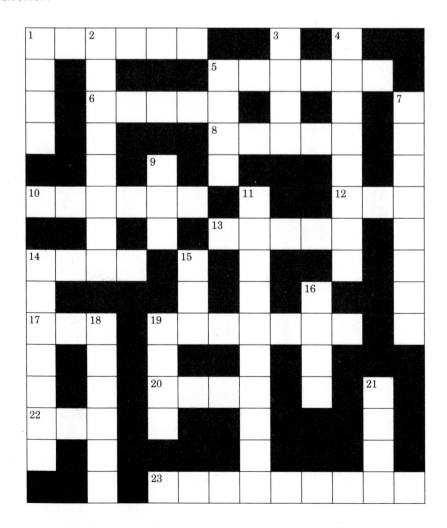